The Grand Spiritual Assumption

Is Salvation really about Heaven?

B. Dale Taliaferro

1

The Grand Spiritual Assumption
Published by Firmly Planted Publications
An imprint of Equipped for Life Ministries

Copyright © 2015 by B. Dale Taliaferro
International Standard Book Number:
978-1-950072-09-5

For information:
Equipped for Life Ministries
P.O. Box 12013
Dallas, Texas 75225
U.S.A.

Library of Congress Control Number:

Revised Edition 2019

Acknowledgements

There are so many threads that God is weaving together to bring me to my current position. There were many books that touched upon either the topic itself or upon tangential issues that strikingly brought out various dilemmas in my current thinking. There were particular authors striving to understand the Scriptures better and willing to courageously challenge the traditional thinking of our day. There are articles and sermons to which I am indebted for shaking up my neat, little, theological world. None of these resources would probably be considered earth-shaking in itself. But all of them kept nibbling away at my understanding of the Bible until I had to admit that I must begin again, starting all over in an attempt to better understand the Bible to which I am so committed. But the practical experiences, that God allowed me to have with many men and women who are just as interested in getting the message of the Bible right, may have played the biggest role in changing my understanding. And in particular, I would like to thank my weekly, men's Bible studies for being traveling down a road filled with potholes and for sticking with me as I would often come in and change some point of teaching that I would have been emphatic about just a couple of years or months earlier. But the clearer we see the Scriptures, the more change in our thinking is inevitable. I am so indebted to these guys for their enduring commitment to seek the truth regardless of how many times we would have to change our minds about it. With all my heart, I thank you.

Dedication

I want to dedicate this book to Dr. Earl Radmacher who just recently went home to be with the Lord. The academic training he provided me, his role modeling of the diligence needed to pursue a better understanding of the Scriptures, his loving friendship, and his interaction of the issues addressed in this book have given me the courage to pursue the Lord who alone leads us into truth. Although he had only read the first volume of this series, calling it a blessing to him, I know that he was also coming to the same conclusions that I have reached herein. If he had lived longer, he would have done a much better job of formulating and communicating these truths. He will be greatly missed because he was so greatly loved.

Table of Contents

Preface to the Revised Edition

This series of books was written during my spiritual journey. As a result, I now find the need to go back through each volume and make some necessary corrections and updates. I really didn't understand how many preconceived ideas that I was working from and that were still hindering my comprehension of the real message of the Bible. I still needed to confront several issues and hold them under the microscope of God's Word. For the sake of simplicity, I will summarize those issues here:

1. I developed a better understanding of the historical situations of some very important passages which changed my thinking relative to their meaning. As a result, the unpardonable sin has been revised. Basically, the unpardonable sin is a rejection of Jesus as the Messiah by the first century Jewish people, resulting in a delay of their earthly kingdom, promised to them by God in the OT, and to their missing entering into that kingdom in their mortal bodies.

2. I finally was able to move past my theological prejudices concerning Acts 16:31 and Eph. 2:8-9 by understanding salvation and faith Biblically. As a result, I have found that the Bible does not describe a person as being saved from hell because salvation never refers to a deliverance from hell once-for-all or in any other way. Consequently, these two classic passages on salvation have nothing to do with a rescue from hell with a promise of heaven. Those ideas have been read into these passages without any substantiation.

3. Since no one was ever described as a "saved person" by *initially* trusting in Jesus, I am led to reframe from do-

1

ing that as well. I eventually realized that even the apostles were not described as "saved persons" after they had initially trusted in Jesus. *Salvation is not a standing or status before God that guarantees a person a heavenly home and an escape from hell.* Nor is it a permanent, unchangeable condition that is reached by initially (or continually) trusting in Jesus. We can be saved from temptations and sins, but we can't be saved from hell and given heaven due to a simple trust in Jesus.

4. Finally, I realized that while there is no concept in the NT that can be likened to the traditional idea of a "saved person" in Christian teachings, there is a NT concept of a *salvation that is taking place presently.* As a result, it is biblical to describe people as being saved from temptations and sins but not as having been saved once for all from hell with a guarantee of heaven. Since the Bible doesn't do that, neither should we. It is easy to see how this reinforces the new understanding of Acts 16:30-31 and Eph. 2:8-9.

With these discoveries, I was able to reach a consistent concept of salvation with nothing but the Bible as my guide. **The biggest correction that I have needed in these volumes is to distinguish between a *spiritual* salvation that is defined as an ongoing deliverance from temptations and sins from the traditional, but mistaken, idea of a *spiritual* salvation that supposedly takes place at the moment of initial faith in Jesus and that supposedly obtains a deliverance from hell**. While the former is clearly Biblical; the latter is a creation by men alone.

Preface

Tradition! In the Christian religion that word usually refers to the Church Creeds or to the study of Historical Theology. Tradition makes most of us feel safe. To a few others it feels more like bondage. Tradition makes us acceptable to others within the tradition we are a part of; it also tends to make us close-minded to those outside of that particular tradition. We stop thinking critically about our own views, and take it for granted that those who differ from us are wrong. So, when we throw around labels like Catholic or Calvinist or Charismatic, we are basically telling others whom they need to avoid. Because they are not of our tradition, they have nothing to offer us in the way of spiritual insights as we continue to accept what we've been taught without really testing its truthfulness.

I remember the interview with Cru my wife and I had when I was about to graduate from the University of Alabama. We had both come from very conservative homes in the Deep South. While my mother was a Pentecostal, I had no contact with or knowledge of that group since I was raised by her sister, who was, of course, my aunt, and by her husband. There were no such churches anywhere near us for me to have gained an acquaintance with their teachings even if I had been so disposed, which I wasn't. I was ignorantly happy within my own tradition. I wasn't interested in any other tradition.

At the interview we were asked about a lot of different issues. We discussed the salary scale for married couples, the possible college placements we could be assigned, and a very general doctrinal statement. There was one question in the doctrinal statement that completely stumped us. The interviewers asked us what our position on speaking in tongues was. Neither my wife nor I had ever heard of such a phenomenon before. So with a bit of divinely inspired wisdom, I asked, "Well, what is Cru's position on that issue?" The committee explained the ministry's position. My wife and I looked at each other and said, "We can agree to that." We still didn't know what speaking in tongues was! But since we had such a strong sense of God's calling to this ministry, we knew it would all work out in the long run. And indeed it did.

I was very fortunate to have a mother who loved me and who was also outside of my own spiritual tradition. From the beginning of our ministry with Cru, my mom and I discussed this issue through many letters. Several times she made outstanding points in favor of the continuing presence and exercise of that spiritual gift. But I learned to do two things throughout our interchange of ideas: 1.) to go for guidance to others who had more knowledge and experience on an issue; and 2.) to test both sides by the Word of God. In the end it would not be the most educated or the most experienced or the most articulate speaker that should convince me on an issue. It would be the one that was in line with all that the Bible said on that particular subject.

Both sides of this issue brought forth verses that seemed to support their convictions. Consequently, I had to become more capable of handling God's Word so that I could discern between who seemed to be right and who was actually right. I finally came to the point of not being swayed by either side. I became convinced that the Bible speaks authoritatively on every issue it addresses. It alone would be my plumb line. In the end, neither the tradition of Cru nor my mom's tradition won the day. The Bible didn't lead me to either side, but rather to a third position that I still hold today.

God has used all of my experiences and training to mold me into the person that I am today. Certainly the wicked aspects of my life are all my own doing, but God has been able to use even those issues to mature me spiritually and draw me closer to Himself. To be quick to bring every issue to the Word of God is partly the result of my spiritual gifting, my spiritual training, and God's leading in my life. All of these things He gave me. To Him belongs all the glory and honor for all things.

I say all that to explain that while it was not easy for me to begin to question the traditions that I was taught in my ministry vocations and in my seminary training, it was beyond difficult to step away from what I had held for so long. After all, the men under whom I received my training were eminent in the field. I would never compare myself to any of them.

But God began to do a new work in my life. And if He had not been in it, I would not have had the strength to separate myself from the traditions that I had been taught. And you should expect the same experience. If some of what we have believed previously is in error, be assured that Satan does not want us to correct it. If truth sets us free, then error binds us even if that binding isn't presently perceivable.

This series of books is the result of God's persistent *goading*. I didn't want to walk down this path, but He would not let me avoid it. As a result I have the greatest expectation that this study will continue to lead you, as the previous two books have tried to do as well, into a greater, moment-by-moment dependence upon the Lord Jesus so that God may be glorified in all that you do. To that end I invite you to join me in this spiritual journey into greater light, an illumination that both clarifies as well as simplifies the teaching of the Bible. The issue at hand is this simple: will we be open to further illumination by the Spirit of God?

But a last word needs to be said about the limitations of all of these books. They are all intended to be studied in the order that they were written and should be considered as successive layers for a new foundation in understanding the message of the Bible. None of these books will cover all the issues that could be addressed when discussing the various topics broached in them. So, in the first book, *The Prodigal Paradigm*, I attempted to demonstrate that the Bible is not a story of God's redemption of man in the sense that we are familiar with. God is not pursing man to rescue him from hell. Rather, *He is pursuing man to help him fulfill his creative purpose of walking with God and representing Him in all that he does*. As a result, there is no evangelistic thrust in the OT at all. God isn't sending anyone, not even His prophets, to anyone, not even the other nations surrounding Israel, to lead them to what we mistakenly call *saving faith*. That is simply one of the incontrovertible facts of the OT. *Our evangelism today is based upon an incorrect view of the message of the Bible.*

There are many tangential issues that were never even brought up in that first book. For example, I said little about the necessity of the peoples of the nations surrounding Israel to believe in Israel's coming Messiah for them to enter into a right relationship with the one, true God. That topic was saved for the second book, *Acceptable to God without being Saved*. Saul, who became the apostle Paul, is the living demonstration of the answer that I would have given if I had addressed it in the first book.

I have chosen to deal with the subjects that need to be discussed in the simplest way possible because these studies will require a great deal of change in our thinking. And, if some of you are like me, you will not be able to take in that much at any given time because the ramifications of each topic can become rather overwhelming. As a result, I have tried to give small bite sized pieces in each book while, hopefully, laying a solid foundation, one layer upon the next. As we move forward, eventually all the issues will be connected together and seen properly.

This book is the third one in the series. It is a discussion on soteriology or the doctrine of salvation. It will surprise you to find how many *assumptions* there are about salvation that are completely unsupportable from the Bible. *It is our theology that has defined salvation for us, not the Bible.* And on this issue, I have discovered that our theology is dreadfully wrong, creating many of the perennial problems we see in the lives of Christians today. We must remember that if truth sets us free, and if error binds us in some way, then the mistaken theology that we have received is keeping us from a full experience of the Spirit of God. It is still true that "where the Spirit of God is, there is freedom," just as the apostle Paul stated in 2Cor. 3:17.

Many related problems to salvation won't be broached in order to keep the study simplified. In fact, most of the chapters will deal with some aspect of salvation that is clearly set forth in in the Scriptures. As we follow the usages of the two terms *save* and *salvation*, these topics will present themselves to us naturally. I am not going to attempt any systematization of related doctrines such as the teaching on ransom, redemption, or reconciliation. What is said about salvation, however, shouldn't be rejected or changed because it doesn't *fit* into some other doctrine.

7

Rather we must understand that the systematization that we have received is some way in error. Our systematization needs to be changed, not the straightforward teaching on salvation as it stands in the Scriptures.

What the Scriptures say about salvation will be accepted to be true, regardless of how other doctrines may have been related in the past to the doctrine of salvation, unwittingly blurring the meaning of salvation for the sake of a smooth, rational systematization of all the related doctrines on soteriology. The reader will be able to confirm each conclusion reached in this study by simply going to the texts cited and reading them for himself. Though the study must be incomplete, there is nothing that is left out that will demand that the conclusions reached here are wrong or misleading. As a result, I urge the reader to wrestle with the things that are addressed without worrying about the things that aren't. All the necessary issues will be covered in one book or the other, or through a different venue altogether, like the new blog that Curtis Tucker and I are setting up. It is called *Maverick Ministers*. Check us out on the internet and ask your questions there if they haven't been answered in our various books.

Introduction

For me it is hard to even hear the word "tradition" without thinking of the movie, *Fiddler on the Roof*. The lead actor, Tevye, opens up the musical with this little monologue spoken right into the camera:

> "A fiddler on the roof. Sounds crazy, no? But here in our little village of Anatevka, you might say everyone of us is a fiddler on the roof, trying to scratch out a pleasant, simple tune without breaking his neck. It isn't easy. You may ask, 'Why do we stay up there if it's so dangerous?' Well, we stay because Anatevka is our home. And how do we keep our balance? That I can tell you in one word: 'Tradition!'"

The entire movie describes the struggle between holding fast to one's traditions and making changes that seem to be for the best as life moves forward and as one's understanding develops. In the words of the lead actor the benefit of tradition is that "everyone of us knows who he is and what God expects him to do." Tradition also, according to Tevye, helps people move through the world without losing their identity. It helps one "keep his balance" in an ever-changing world.

But there are also major problems with tradition. Not only can the meaning of the traditions be lost, but long-standing traditions may become unassailable and above all possible critique simply because they have been held for so long. Tevye explains this for us when he says,

> "Here in Anatevka, we have traditions for everything: how to sleep, how to eat, how to work, how to wear clothes. For instance, we always keep our heads covered, and always wear a little prayer shawl. ***This shows our constant devotion***

to God. You may ask, how did this tradition get started? I'll tell you. I don't know. But it's a tradition." (emphasis mine)

We must understand the relation between a tradition and a command from the Lord. If God commands something, that settles the issue entirely. It is to be done without hesitation with a whole heart. But if the tradition is an invention of man in order to facilitate the obedience to God's commands, the tradition can be ignored or set aside entirely, but the command must continue to be obeyed until God sets it aside by His own doing.

Both the *kippah* and the prayer shawl are religious developments by the Jewish people as aids for keeping God's commands. But the wearing of these items of clothing are not commanded by the Scriptures. The fringed garment that is commanded in the Scriptures for the Jewish people was a reminder to obey the commandments of God, not to pray.

We must hold fast to this distinction between a tradition and a command of Scripture. It doesn't matter if the tradition is a garment of clothing or a doctrinal formulation by religious leaders. The all-important issue is whether the activity or obligation or doctrine in question is required by the Scriptures or not.

Unfortunately, traditions are usually taken as a set of timeless and unchanging doctrines handed down from one generation to the next. They become over time representative of the requirements of God for understanding His will properly and for the practice of it in a way that is sure to please Him. As Jesus taught His disciples, however, religious traditions may actually set aside or nullify God's Word so that it is not only not practiced, but also hidden from view entirely. *Religious traditions may replace God's Word rather than represent it to His people.* This is true with doctrines as well as practices.

Religious standards should not be changed whenever the culture around it changes. That is backwards! God's word is unchanging and ought to be the catalyst for changing the culture, not the other way around. But the way we create unchanging traditions and allow them to masquerade as commands of God gives us little hope in changing anything. In fact, *Christianity seems to be more irrelevant to a changing world each year.*

After Tevye violated his traditions on behalf of his first two daughters for the sake of their future marital happiness, he finds that he can go no further without denying who he is as a Jew. He finds himself locked into certain traditions that are mistakenly thought to represent God's will for his life. If he approved of his third daughter's marriage to a Gentile, a Russian soldier, who symbolizes all those who have ruled over the Jews from ancient times into the twenty-first century, he would directly transgress the Jewish laws on marriage. The love for his daughter was great, but the love for his faith was even greater. So, he confesses,

"If I try and bend that far, I'll break."

At that point he chooses to cling to his faith regardless of the consequences his steadfast stand on tradition will have on his relationship with his daughter. By being committed to a false understanding of his faith, he forfeits many of God's blessings intended for his happiness.

Fiddler on the Roof ends before we discover how Tevye's and Chava's disagreement mars their relationship and affects their personal lives. But the loss of personal intimacy between those who obviously loved each other so much was so unnecessary. If only they had had the courage to question the tradition that was tearing them apart.

11

Freeing believers from the bondage of extra-biblical or un-biblical traditions is part of the reason that I am writing this book. We have arbitrarily limited God in how He can work and have reaped the consequences of confining God in this way. A large part of those consequences is that we have missed the blessings that would have come from the various relationships that we have ignored or not sought. And we have ignored and not sought them for no other reason than that our traditions have restrained us from them. Like Tevye we lost those cherished relationships. Unlike Tevye we don't have any idea how precious they actually are.

This book will attempt to challenge several doctrines that are considered orthodox because of how long they have been held. But we will clearly demonstrate that their long-accepted status will not shield them from the fact that they are man-made without any support from the Scriptures. I hope what is said here will not offend any reader. Rather I hope that it will challenge each one to return to his personal study of the Scriptures in order to test not only what he is reading, but also what he has been taught. May such renewed study draw you even closer to the God who has revealed Himself to you in so many ways already.

Chapter 1

A Call for Courage!

My wife and I went into the ministry right out of college. To describe us as novices would be an understatement. But we had a heart for God, a teachable spirit, and a very clear calling from God. So, off we went. That decision was one of the five or six that I have experienced in my life in which the leading of the Lord was so strong that I didn't really believe there was any alternative that I could choose and be, at the same time, really following God. In my case, I didn't want to choose any other profession because my heart was so fully set upon ministry by God's gracious presence and leading in my life.

After our first year on staff with Cru, the senior staff woman at our college campus asked me to read a book that she found quite troubling. The title of the book was *The Reformed Doctrine of Predestination*, written by L. Boettner. It is considered a classic work on predestination and election, and is still a well-respected book in the field of theology today.

Like I said before, I was a novice in ministry, having no formal seminary education at that point. But I loved God's Word and had a passion to share my faith and disciple those who wanted to grow in the Christian faith. While I was certainly a novice, I had, nevertheless, a . . . *fruitful* mind. I suppose that is what I should call it. I would never compare myself to those who taught me or to those older than I was and with more experience than I had. I knew my place in the world and was happy to be useful to God in whatever position He chose for me.

So, when Sheila gave me that book to critique, I thought to myself, "I'm not sure I can do this. But OK. She is troubled over it so I'll do the best I can." After reading the book, I told Sheila not to let it bother her any longer. I could offer alternative explanations to every verse used in the book except one. These alternatives were not created in the spirit of antagonism. They sprang from seeking an interpretation that would reflect the context of the Biblical author's original statements. Consequently, I told her that if I could see genuine alternatives to the theological interpretation of the passages suggested by Boettner, imagine what a trained person would say.

We were both relieved for the present. But at the end of that second year of ministry, I felt God leading once again. This time to seminary. After my first year in seminary, I found myself in the same turmoil that Sheila had been in the previous year because I was taking a class that, among other topics, was covering the doctrine of election and predestination. Having such a high regard for my professors, I concluded that I had been wrong on this subject and needed to accept the account that was being presented to me. I did that even though it caused both my wife and me great turmoil and a lot of sleepless nights.

But after cramming a four-year seminary program into five years, and after further seminary training on the doctoral level, along with about twenty-five years of ministry experience, I begin to revisit all of these issues again. And to my amazement, I began to return to the conclusions that I had reached over thirty years previously *before* I had gone to seminary. It took me that long to see the need to question what I had been taught. But fortunately, part of my seminary education trained me to do just that. Of course, initially I had applied my training to the critique of those who differed from what I had been taught. But in God's good timing I began to see the need to question my own views as well.

This book is the third in a series of at least five books that reevaluates central doctrines that have formed the basis for our understanding of the Bible. The first book, *The Prodigal Paradigm*, challenges the idea that the Bible is about a *redemptive plan* of God, taking *redemptive* in the contemporary sense of being saved from hell. I found that the Bible isn't about that at all. It is about *God pursuing those whom He had created to bring them back to Himself for fellowship and service in order for them to represent Him in all that they do.*

The second book, *Acceptable to God without Being Saved*, uses the man Saul, who became the apostle Paul, to illustrate all of the principles that were suggested in the first book. **Men exist who are acceptable to God but who have not trusted in Jesus.** While there are numerous Biblical examples of this fact, I picked Saul because he lived *after* Jesus' ministry, *after* His death and resurrection, and *after* the Jewish church began to experience an unprecedented growth. Because he comes after Jesus's life and ministry, he establishes the possibility that such people as he was may still exist today, such people as *those who are acceptable to God without being saved, in the traditional sense, by Jesus.*

This book will suggest that the common *assumption* about salvation being a deliverance from hell and into heaven is impossible to find in the Scriptures unless *conjectures* and *assumptions* are layered one on top of the next to insert it there. It is a fact that there is no verse that simply tells a person to believe in Jesus in order to escape hell. Neither is there a verse that plainly tells a person to believe in Jesus in order to gain heaven. Not one. Doesn't that surprise you . . . just a bit?

But it's . . . tradition! It's what we have always been taught. But that doesn't make it right. But I'm getting ahead of myself.

I have had the privilege of knowing and sitting under the teaching of both Dr. Howard Blandeau and Dr. Henry Brandt. Both were eminent psychologists who understood that any psychological theory that contradicted the Bible had to be, in the nature of the case, incorrect. Dr. Brandt's story demonstrates how tradition, even though it might have been passed down through the academic halls of our universities and seminaries, can be so far afield that the truth has actually been hidden by it.

Dr. Brandt was an engineer by profession. But because of his evident wisdom, gained by his own personal study of God's Word, he was usually inundated with requests for counseling. After years of personal counseling and because he enjoyed helping people so much, he decided to go back to school and get a doctorate in psychology. It took him eight long years to fulfill all the requirements for that degree. But he finally got it.

Then he began counseling full time, using all the latest information that he had been taught in the doctoral program. But a problem arose. Before he got his degree and when he simply used the principles that he had learned from God's Word, he had remarkable success in leading people to changed lives and successful living. But now the fruits of his labor seemed to have dried up almost entirely.

At this point he made the decision to go back to this former basis for counseling, the Bible. In his own personal testimony, he liked to say,

"It took me eight years to get my doctorate in psychology, but it took me ten years to flush out of my thinking all that training so that I could once again help people."

While that is a paraphrase of what I heard more than once while in his presence, the essence of it is true to fact.

What was true of Dr. Brandt in the field of psychology was also true of me in the field of theology. The more I got back to the Bible and forgot the theological grid that I had been taught, the clearer the Bible became, and my perspective on all of life was transformed. But until I became willing to start over and test the validity of the theological consensus, I kept having the same problem: finding lots of verses that simply didn't fit the interpretations or the system that I had been taught. Those passages that were so problematic simply wouldn't go away. And as they seemed for some divine purpose to pop up more readily than before, their challenge to my neat little system became sharper and more troubling each time I had to address them.

The Bible is very clear that *the culture or tradition in which a person has been raised may shout down the voice of God, nullifying the educational and transformational affects it was meant to effect.* When dealing with the subject of Christian Liberty ~ making decisions on culturally explosive but amoral issues ~ Paul warned how strongly culture can influence each person's receptivity:

> "However not all men have this knowledge; but some, *being accustomed* to the idol until now, eat food as if it were sacrificed to an idol; and their conscience, being weak, is defiled." (1Cor. 8:7)

Since everyone is culturally conditioned, it is crucial to test every tradition and doctrine by God's Word. If we don't do that, our traditions might keep us from God's truth just as the Corinthians' culture kept them from understanding God's grace.

In a very similar way, doctrines have been formulated, un-

17

wittingly I have no doubt, by Christian leaders who have gone before us, that either hinder, limit, or nullify completely what God is actually saying to us through His written Word. What if, for example, eternal life is not at all about eternity but is rather a resource that Jesus gives for people today to live an abundant life in fellowship with God throughout each day? Instead of focusing on eternity, our focus would change to daily living and the importance that kind of living has for our experience after death. No longer would people be more concerned about "getting to heaven" than they would be about living the kind of life now that God requires. You could take forgiveness in exactly the same way.

So, I'm asking the reader to have the courage to set aside all that he has learned and start from scratch. You have accepted the word of trusted theologians up to this point. Now I'm asking you to trust the Spirit of God to illumine you as you study the Scriptures on your own, taking them literally as each context demands. If you will do that, you will find an entirely different message being proclaimed in God's Word. And it is *that message* that God wants us to believe and to proclaim to the whole world.

Chapter 2

Incontrovertible Facts

When I was very young, there was a weekly TV series called *Dragnet*. The star of the show was a police sergeant named Joe Friday. Every time he had the task of interviewing those involved in the crime or who had witnessed the crime, he would say,

"Just the facts, Ma'am (or Sir), just the facts."

With that statement he was trying to keep the person being interviewed from drawing any conclusions about what happened. Drawing conclusions from the facts was his job as an impartial investigator. If we took Sergeant Friday's approach to the study of the Scriptures, what conclusions would we draw about the teachings of the Bible?

Well, first we need to uncover the facts. What are they? And it is important that we begin with just the obvious, incontrovertible facts. As I list *some* of these facts, I will mention briefly a few ideas that make them so important. But these are the facts that have been uncovered from my own personal study.

The incontrovertible truths listed here do not come from any particular denomination. They are listed here only because I have not found in my investigation of the Bible's use of these terms any exceptions to them. If we allow these facts to have the impact upon our worldview as God intended, we will gain an insight into reality that we did not have before. You will have to struggle, as I did, to overcome your *preconceptions* about some of these truths. But I offer nothing more than the conclusions that I have reached after investigating the Biblical crime scene.

1. Salvation is *never* connected to *initial faith* in the OT.

> Never is *initial* faith set before the reader as the cause or the immediately preceding condition for any kind of *spiritual* salvation, that is, *a deliverance from hell* and a provision of heaven (as the old paradigm teaches). Salvation, in that sense, is never broached in the OT or the NT. And yet God clearly tells us that the whole Jewish nation throughout its OT history was considered *His first born son, His chosen people.*[1] There is an on-going spiritual salvation that occurs daily which is never connected to initial faith ~ if there is such a thing (see the next point below).

2. In fact, there is no example of *initial faith* in the OT at all.

> If *initial* faith could be found (to this point, I have failed to find it), it would never be described as, or connected to, the *spiritual* salvation from hell taught in traditional Christian theology. Now you must ask yourself, "If the Bible doesn't give a *starting point* at which a person begins a relationship with God, how can anyone determine what is supposed to happen at that mysterious and undisclosed starting point?"
>
> Have you been taught that lots of things happened to a person the moment he *first* believes? How can such a statement be made if there is not one instance of *initial faith* in God in the whole OT? How could anyone know what happens at initial faith if there is no passage that actually addresses that subject and *explicitly* tells the reader what happens then? *Initial faith in Jesus is not the same thing as initial faith in God.* More of that topic later.

---

[1] Isa. 1:1-4. See my book *The Prodigal Paradigm* for a sufficient proof of this point.

3. Salvation and justification are *never synonymous.*

These two phenomena are not the same thing; they do not occur at the same time; nor do they secure heaven as a guaranteed destiny. All of those ideas are *assumed* to be true without any *explicit confirmation* of them from the Scriptures.

4. Justification is *not a once-for-all matter* in the Bible.

Although most of us have been taught that justification is a once-for-all event, the life of Abraham clearly teaches us otherwise. Abraham was justified twice in the Scriptures to teach us that justification is not a one-time issue. *In fact, Abraham's case teaches us that the entire forensic paradigm that we placed on top of justification is incorrect.* Abraham's justification was not the declaration of a judge, even of a divine Judge, concerning his guilt or innocence or of his status or standing before God legally.

Abraham's justification was the declaration of a Father who has complete authority over His household to regulate the standard by which His family must live. When His children do the right thing, He *justifies* their deed, declaring it to be a response well done. When they do the wrong thing, He *condemns* their deed, declaring it to be worthless. The forensic paradigm has blinded us to the fact that God is a loving, heavenly Father who seeks to draw all men back into fellowship with Him in order to worship and serve Him.

5. No one is described as *spiritually saved* in the OT.

This is another incontrovertible fact that will astonish a lot of Christians who have only heard the term salvation used to describe a deliverance from hell. Not one time is Adam and Eve, or Abel, or Seth, or Noah, or Job, or Abraham, or Isaac,

21

or Jacob, or any of his twelve sons, including Joseph, or David, or Daniel, or any of the prophets ever described as a *spiritually saved person* (saved from hell) *who became so at some point in his life by one response of faith*. Why would that be?

The answer is as obvious as it is hidden from view in the theology that has been handed down to us from Augustine through the Reformation. They were not described as spiritually saved from hell because they weren't! Spiritual salvation (i.e., the traditional Christian concept of an escape from hell) is not a truth *explicitly* found in the Scriptures. Reading this doctrine into either the NT the OT has distorted the message of the Bible.

6. *Initial faith* (or any other faith) in Jesus in the NT is never directly related to heaven or hell.

Are you surprised by this fact? I was! Since going to heaven and escaping hell was always presented to me as the result of believing in Jesus, I assumed that connection was beyond debate. But Jesus *never* offers this result to those He invites to trust in Him. The connection between faith in Jesus and both the attainment of heaven along with the escape from hell comes from the Augustinian-Reformed concept of forensic pardon or guilt. If a person is pardoned, he goes free (and thereby gets to go to heaven). If he is found guilty, he is condemned (and as a result is sentenced to an eternity in hell). This, they told us, was the meaning of justification and condemnation in the Scriptures.

As I have already shown in my book, *The Prodigal Paradigm*, and mentioned again above, justification has nothing to do with such a forensic concept at all. It concerns how life is lived: is it lived in a manner pleasing to God or is it lived in a way that He must temporally condemn? Neither concept has anything to do with a person's permanent standing or status before God. Both justification and condemnation are practical, describing how life is being lived, not how God is determining a person's eternal destiny.

7. Salvation is *never* directly related to heaven or hell.

Yes, this is a redundant statement. But it was added because of the confusion about salvation generally. While Jesus does offer *salvation* to the person who believes in Him, that salvation has to do with this life, not with eternity. *Jesus never offered a free trip to heaven based upon a once-for-all response of faith in Him.*

If salvation only denotes in your mind the attainment of heaven and the escape from hell, and if you are trusting in that alone to stand before the throne, you may be in for an enormous shock. The salvation that Jesus offered was a deliverance from the personal responses (sins) that fail to qualify as the righteousness that gains entrance into the kingdom when it is finally established. We have been offered *a new life* by Jesus that can fulfill, motivate, and bring a new purpose to our souls. That gift of life will not by itself gain us entrance into kingdom of heaven though. But it will enable us to get there after we have had an extraordinary walk with God, experiencing it on a daily basis.

8. Many *"believers"* in the OT didn't persevere in their faith.

First of all, notice that I emphasized the term *believer*. I did that because no one is called *a believer* in the OT. Certainly, one can find many who believed in the one, true God in the OT. But that is not the point. The point is that we have taken the term *believer* and poured into it a theological library of meaning, most of which it cannot carry.

The idea of *believer* ought to be limited to the concept of a person who, at a given point in time, is either believing God or he is not believing God (so that he would then be defined as an *unbeliever* in that instance). The terms *believer* and *unbeliever* do not describe two easily identified groups of persons, one of which is destined for heaven while the other is bound for hell. The nouns (or rather the substantival adjectives) aren't used until one gets all the way to 1Corinthians in the NT. In our attempts to systematize the Scriptures, we have done a great deal of disservice to various terms and to various Greek constructions.

The fact that many believers in the OT don't persevere in their faith is important in itself. It should lead us to question several doctrines that we have been taught. For example, since there are *believers in God* who do not want God to rule over them,[1] either the Scriptures must be given up as our rule of faith or the doctrine of perseverance must be evaluated as false. King Solomon is the poster-child for a person who didn't persevere in his faith to the end of his life.[2]

The doctrine of faith is another teaching that must undergo more scrutiny. Is faith man's responsibility, or is it a gift from God? Since it can fail, it seems rather uncharacteristic for it to be God's gift, especially since the doctrine comes from a theological system that puts so much emphasis on the sovereignty of God.

All three of these doctrines are Biblical doctrines, but

---

[1] 1Sam. 8:4-22.
[2] 1Kgs. 11:1-13.

they have been connected to each other improperly because they are part of a system that depends upon errant connections. It is time to start over.

9. Belief in a coming Messiah *never* guaranteed heaven.

Believing in a coming Messiah was never related to *spiritual salvation* (from hell) in the OT. No one in the OT was urged to believe in the promised Messiah (or in anything that He would do) in order to be *spiritually saved* in the sense of going to heaven and escaping hell. The connection between believing in Jesus and being saved can be found in the NT, but that salvation is never from hell.

In an attempt to systematize the teachings of the Scriptures, errant conclusions have been drawn which are not benign. They can lead to confusion and false hope. We must be content in reading the Bible forward and not reading the NT back into the OT unless it is *explicitly* explaining what an OT passage meant. This explanatory function of the NT is a lot rarer than most think.

10. Believing in a coming Messiah was *never* related to the forgiveness of sins in the OT.

Now this is indeed a stunning revelation, is it not? But the surprise is caused by our past programing. We have been taught that believing in a coming Messiah was how a person was *spiritually saved* from hell in the OT. At the moment a person is saved, he is *supposedly forgiven* of all of his sins. But when we find no passage that directs a person to believe in the coming Messiah in order to be saved and/or to be forgiven of his sins, we experience cognitive dissidence. We have trouble making sense out of that information. Being forgiven by believing in the coming Messiah is simply not taught in the OT at all.

When we come to the NT, there is considerable explanation needed on both accounts since we find persons who already believed in the coming Messiah but who were *not yet saved*[1] (in the sense that Jesus offered His salvation), and others who believed in the Jesus but who needed *no forgiveness of sins*.[2] What we have been taught fits a forensic paradigm well, but it fits the actual teaching of the Bible poorly. And sadly, this teaching can't be patched up any more than a piece of shrunk clothing can be patched by a piece of unshrunken cloth, or an old wine skin (of the forensic paradigm) can contain the actual teaching of the Bible.[3]

11. Jesus' death on the cross is *never* directly related to heaven or hell.

Jesus didn't die so those who believe in Him could go to heaven. *This supposition is probably the main idea that drives the teaching about the substitutionary death of Jesus.* He died in our place so that we don't have to die eternally. But if Jesus' death is never directly related to going to heaven or escaping hell, how do we know that a substitutionary theory of the death of Christ is any better than any other theory? Since our next book will be devoted to examining the death of Christ, I will only say here that regardless of what theory one holds to be the best view of the purpose of Christ's death, *no view*

---

[1] Cf., John 4:25-26, 39-42. The fact is that nobody in the entire Bible was *saved* in the traditional Christian sense of escaping hell and being given heaven in hell's place when he believed in the coming Messiah or in Jesus while He ministered for four years. *Salvation* never describes that sort of deliverance.

[2] Cf., Lk. 5:32; 15:7; John 9:1-3, 35-38.

[3] Mk. 2:21-22.

ought to guarantee more than what the Bible specifically gives him the authority to guarantee.

12. Jesus' death is *never* related to the forgiveness of sins that is, *supposedly*, needed to attain heaven.

The incontrovertible fact number ten suggested what is here affirmed. While it is clear that Jesus' death deals with both the (indwelling) sin issue as well as the sins a person actually commits, these benefits do not contribute in any way to the obtainment of a guaranteed, heavenly destiny. But this guarantee is exactly what is *assumed* to be available by believing in Jesus. If there is no place that states the matter in those terms, how do we know that the forgiveness of sins results in the obtainment of heaven? How do we know that belief in Jesus even obtains *any* forgiveness at all? Can we find this truth on the lips of Jesus?

Because of the large number of *assumptions* that we have been taught and have received as true, we now have brain freeze. It is almost impossible for us to begin to think outside the theological box that has been passed down to us. And I understand the problem well because I had to fight the same battles that many of you are beginning to fight now. But if we begin with the *explicit* statements of Scripture and deal with one issue at a time, we can make progress. Jesus' death does relate to forgiveness of sins. But the question is this: in what way does it relate to forgiveness? That question will be dealt with in detail in the next volume in this series.

13. Forgiveness of *all sins at one point* is ever offered, even for faith in Jesus.

Believe it or not, the student of Scripture is actually hard pressed to produce verses that connect forgiveness to believing in Jesus. Think about these points for a moment:

- The Gospel of John, supposedly an evangelistic book, never uses the terms for *forgiveness* or *forgive*. Why is that? It is *supposedly* the Gospel of spiritual salvation (from hell), right? It is the book on eternal life. But no mention of forgiveness being needed. Interesting.
- Were not people forgiven in the OT without reference to the coming Messiah? If God is righteous in offering forgiveness in the OT *apart from faith in the Messiah*, would He be righteous in doing that during the ministry of Jesus or today as well?
- Can you find any passage that says that belief in Jesus takes away *all* of a person's *sins*, those that are past, those that are present, and those that are future?
- Can you find a verse that distinguishes in plainly stated terms the forgiveness of the *eternal penalty* that is *supposed* to be resting upon every sin committed from the forgiveness of the *temporal consequences* of those sins? The point here is this: *how do we know that there is an eternal penalty upon man's sins?* Is this an *assumption* based upon a myriad of additional *assumptions* concerning faith, forgiveness, and hell? When are we going to plant our feet firmly upon the straightforward statements of God's Word?

I found only three verses that even have the possibility of connecting forgiveness to faith in Jesus. None of these actually support the idea that all of the sins a person has or will commit are forgiven in that one-time belief in Jesus. The facts are these: 1.) there *can be* forgiveness obtained when Jesus is trusted in initially; and 2.) there *may not be* any forgiveness obtained when Jesus is trusted in initially. *It appears that only the sins related to an initial rejection of Jesus are forgiven when Je-*

sus is trusted in initially. All other sins are taken away graciously as a person pursues God. Different means may be required by God for different peoples at different times in history to receive the forgiveness that He has graciously provided. But believing in a coming Messiah or in Jesus the Messiah who has finally come is not one of them.

14. Eternal life is *never defined* in relation to eternity.

It is quite common to *assume* that the reception of eternal life is the same as obtaining a guaranteed eternal destiny in heaven. But that *assumption* once again is pure *conjecture*. Furthermore, we know that there were OT persons who gained a heavenly destiny, and yet they were neither saved (in the Christian theological sense) nor did they ever have eternal life. Abraham, Isaac, and Jacob are enough to make this point.[1] The Bible *never defines* eternal life as the gift of a heavenly destiny. When we accept what eternal life actually is, the debate between duration and quality of life will come to an end. *Eternal life is the actual, communicable life of Jesus Christ to man.*[2] Think on that!

15. The kingdom of heaven can't be a synonym for salvation.

Jesus plainly told His apostles that the kingdom could not be established until He, the nobleman of His own parable, left in order to obtain it from the Father and then return.[3] *There is no kingdom until Jesus' return to earth at His second advent.* The salvation that could be gained during His personal ministry, while kingdom related, is broader than the kingdom and has

---

[1] Cf., Matt. 22:31-32.
[2] John 6:47; 14:27; 15:9-10, 11; 16:12-15; Eph. 3:16-17; Gal. 2:20; Rom. 8:37; etc.
[3] Lk. 19:11-12.

nothing to do with obtaining a heavenly destiny. As a result, no one enters the kingdom when he believes in Jesus. No one escapes hell or gains heaven. The salvations that he can have are those related to his rescue from personal sins and temptations and from indwelling sin as well.

16. The gospel is *never* directly connected to heaven or hell.

There is no verse that sets *the gospel* forth as an invitation to heaven or as the possible evasion of hell. Where have you seen a verse that says in essence "This is the good news, the gospel, that by believing in Jesus you will be given a place in heaven"? This connection is reached by rather torturous and circuitous reasoning such as this: "By believing in Jesus you will be saved, that is, you will receive eternal life which is a place in heaven." Or this: "By doing the will of God, which is actually believing in Jesus, you will enter the kingdom of God, which is actually heaven itself." Or this: "By believing that Jesus died for your sins and that, thereby, He has paid for and removed the eternal penalty resting upon your sins, you can have a place in heaven." Have you ever found a verse that puts all these *supposed* truths together without the need for any conjecture? I haven't.

17. The salvation that Jesus offered was accompanied with warnings about going into Gehenna or into the eternal fire.

The most popular way to circumvent this problem is to suggest that such warnings are really hypothetical. But if *we* are able to figure out the warnings are really nothing more than hypothetical motivations to live righteously, why couldn't *the apostles* have figured it out too? And if they had figured it out, the warning would no longer be effective, right? So the salvation that Jesus offered was no guarantee to a person that he would miss the eternal fires of Gehenna.

If the facts listed above are too hard to follow, let me draw a bigger, more general picture for you. *Jesus never gave a message that could be summarized as an invitation for a person to believe in Him so that he could go to heaven and escape hell.* The twelve apostles never gave such a message either. Nor did the apostle Paul.

So how in the world did we get such a message? We got it by following the *systematic conclusions of men* who did not do justice to the facts of Scripture. If Sergeant Joe Friday were here today, he would be constantly repeating his well-known and highly anticipated line: "Just the facts, Sirs, just the facts."

The Bible is setting forth God's desire for all of His creatures to walk with Him. When they do, they are blessed. When they don't, they are cursed.[1] And, indeed, according to the Scriptures, **any man**, regardless of the nation where he lives or the religion that he believes, who

> "fears God and does what is right *is acceptable to* (or welcomed by) *Him*." (Acts 10:34-35, my translation)

This was the lesson that Peter learned when he was sent to preach Jesus to Cornelius. And Peter was referring to Cornelius when he made that statement. In other words, *Cornelius was already acceptable to God **before** he ever heard the message about Jesus!*[2]

These are the facts that I uncovered in my own investigations of the Scriptures. If you use a simple English concordance, you will reach the same conclusions. The rest of this book will help us understand how all of these facts impact our perspective

---

[1] Cf., Deut. 27-28 for an understanding of both God's blessing and His cursing.
[2] Acts 10:22, 34, 35

on life and on all of the relationships that exist in it.

Chapter 3

Words!

When my children were very little, their understanding had to develop so they could effectively communicate to my wife and me. Sometimes what they thought they heard wasn't exactly what was being said. So, for the term kitchen, they would say, "chetchen." And for ketchup, they would say, "chetzchup." And "minnamine," we eventually figured out, meant grapefruit, and "howhouse" was a reference to flowers. Some of their words we could comprehend immediately; others were not so evident. But to the uninitiated person to our little family culture, many words simply did not communicate meaningfully at all.

When Shannon, my daughter, was a little girl, she thought her hair shampoo was called "Shannonpoo" instead of shampoo. So, one day she asked us if her brother's hair shampoo was called "Ryanpoo" (since his name is Ryan).

Then came the day when we were caravanning back from a ministry activity. When we stopped to eat dinner, Shannon got out of the car and almost immediately came running up to her mom, who, I am glad to say, is still after 50 years my wife, shouting, "Mommy, Mommy, my 'brains' are falling out! My 'brains' are falling out!" Waunee had put her hair into braids. One of the braids was slipping out of place. While the words are identical except for one letter, their meanings are worlds apart.

But probably my favorite verbal mix-up happened at the time my family went to a backyard baptism at a private home in their swimming pool. One of the young girls who was going to be baptized was having a pool party afterwards so she had invited several of her school friends to come to her baptism. Her friends had already donned their bathing suits in preparation for the party after the baptismal ceremony. One of the little girls was wearing a bikini, a bathing suit that my daughter had seen on others but did not have herself. She whispered into Waunee's ear, "Mommy, she (pointing to the little girl in the bikini) is wearing a 'zucchini!'" Close enough, you say? True, for innocent conversations.

I suppose most families have stories like these. Children learn by hearing in context. Sometimes they connect the wrong words, that they think they have heard others use, to describe certain objects or concepts. Then, these words that have been associated with particular objects or concepts become the established means of talking about those objects and concepts.

In the same way, we learn the doctrines of the Bible as we listen to others discuss them. We hear the words they use to describe those doctrines, and those words soon take on a life of their own. Whenever they are heard again, they are naturally associated with the doctrines that were being discussed when they were first heard. The words that we are concerned with in this chapter are *salvation* and *save*.

It is ingrained into our thinking from an early age that *salvation* refers to the guarantee of a heavenly destiny and an escape from hell. Salvation becomes so connected with "going to heaven" and "escaping hell" that it is almost impossible to think of that term in any other way. Consequently, when we talk about being *saved*, it is to this heavenly attainment and fiery escape that we refer.

As we proceed in our discussions of these terms, the reader is urged to retreat to a complete concordance of the Bible as often as he feels the need in order to check particular passages on salvation or on being saved. We ought not to continue to believe anything that can't be grounded in the Bible's actual use of these terms. When we call things by the wrong term, as when my daughter called a bikini a zucchini, we lose the real meaning of one term and mischaracterize the other term.

The Meaning of Salvation

I thought all the mispronounced words by my children, growing up, were so cute. It was very hard to correct them at times because part of me wanted the mispronounced words or the misunderstood terms to continue in their vocabulary because they were so charming and precious. But at some point for their good and the good of sound communication, correction was needed and had to be administered.

As you search the usages of the noun, *salvation*, and the verb, *save*, in your concordance, you will discover to your utter amazement that there is not one instance of these terms referring to heaven or to hell. To put it simply: *being saved does not mean being kept from hell, nor does salvation refer to a destiny in heaven.* My daughter's reference to her braided hair as her brains mischaracterized her hair, calling it something it wasn't, and, at the same time, the true meaning of her brain was lost. By giving the term *salvation* the wrong definition or referent, that term's true meaning and referent may be lost forever.

If salvation refers to going to heaven and escaping hell, and if salvation is obtained only through faith in Jesus, then everyone who fails to believe in Jesus, for whatever reason, misses out on heaven. This is the view of most Christians today. *But if salvation doesn't refer to going to heaven and escaping hell, then failing to believe in Jesus does not put a person in jeopardy of hell nor does believing in Jesus secure heaven.*

You see, our current understanding of the concept of salvation is actually a *presumption* that has no Biblical support to enable it to withstand close scrutiny. The currently accepted meaning of salvation springs from circuitous reasoning that opens the doors for sleight-of-hand eisegesis (reading one's theology into the text of Scripture when it really isn't there). To be convinced that those who believe in Jesus get to go to heaven and those who fail to believe in Jesus are left out cannot be proven from a straightforward reading of the Bible.

As you read this discussion on salvation, can you think of any verse that says straightforwardly "if you believe in Jesus, you will go to heaven," or "if you reject Jesus, you will go to hell"? I've not found one verse that says that. Not one. As a result, this truth makes the list of those incontrovertible facts of the Scriptures given earlier. We must believe those facts or go astray. Praise God because He ever waits for us to come back!

I'm not a student of historical theology for a lot of reasons. But mostly it is due to my own lack of study in that discipline. I do love the Bible, however, and I have studied it intently for the last forty-five years. When I find no verse that simply states that believing in Jesus is the means of obtaining a place in heaven and when I find no verse that warns a person that failing to believe in Jesus is the means of losing any hope of heaven, I pause and ask, "How can that be? All the discussions I've ever heard from the Christian ranks pontificate that Jesus is the only way to heaven." In fact, those ranks assure me that heaven is guaranteed to everyone who has "truly believed in Jesus."

If Jesus were the only way to heaven, wouldn't you suppose that there would be plenty of verses supporting such a claim? Rather, what we hear from those who adhere to this belief are circuitous arguments that are a lot like the draw-by-dots books my children use to enjoy. The desired picture would come into view only after lots of dots had been connected.

In the same way, since there is no direct, simple statement in the Scriptures that actually says that believing in Jesus gains heaven for a person, the proponent of that doctrine has to connect lots of dots that *supposedly* lead to that conclusion. But the question remains, "Do those connected theological dots really reveal the picture being desired?"

Likewise, there is no direct, simple statement that failing to believe in Jesus makes heaven unreachable. Rather, this position is reached by *supposing* that other promises, such as the offer of eternal life to the one who believes in Jesus, are basically synonymous to the *supposed* promise of heaven that Jesus gives to each person who believes in Him. But have these supposed equivalents been proven to us? Is *being saved* and is *receiving eternal life* really about the attainment of heaven? Or is this just another assumption without the supportive, Biblical proof that is necessary to be convincing?

But equating believing in Jesus for a guaranteed ticket to heaven and obtaining eternal life for a guaranteed place with Jesus in eternity only establishes the fact that this position is based upon yet another *assumption*: that eternal life is a reference to heaven. Since eternal life and heaven are never equated in the Scriptures, all of these *presumed* identifications are nothing more than wishful *assumptions*. And soon we find ourselves literally

layered with presupposition after presupposition and with conjecture after conjecture.

What is being taught may sound very reasonable and may
be most soothing to our anxious hearts. But those aren't the cri-
teria we should be using to accept a teaching as true. One thing,
and one thing alone, ought to be demanded by us: a Biblical
foundation for the teaching in question.

Chapter 4

Salvation is Multi-Faceted

We've discussed what the terms salvation and save do not mean. Now we must uncover what they do mean.

In the movie *How to Steal a Million*, Audrey Hepburn plays Nicole Bonnet, the daughter of a very wealthy art collector, who also happens to be an art forger, and Peter O'Toole plays Simon Dermott, an insurance investigator, doubling as a thief in order to catch Mr. Charles Bonnet, Hepburn's father, in the act of reproducing or selling his forgeries as priceless works of art. Unknowingly Nicole, who has always disapproved of her father's production of forgeries, fearing that one day he may get caught and sent to jail, recruited Simon to help her steal a small statue called the Cellini Venus. The statue actually belonged to her father, but she had to steal it before it could be technically examined by the museum to which it had been loaned as the centerpiece of an important art exhibition. If it was examined, everyone would discover that it was a fake, throwing suspicion upon Mr. Bonnet's entire art collection.

After the great heist of the Cellini Venus had been successfully accomplished, Nicole and Simon were meeting for breakfast at the Ritz Bar. Nicole was extremely excited about their success since her father is now in the clear. She tells Simon that she hoped that she had been some help in the heist even though it was her first "caper." In response Simon said, "Mine too," by which he meant that this was his first caper or robbery as well.

Nicole looks at him inquisitively with disbelief because she had caught him in her house *apparently* trying to steal one of their paintings. From that encounter she *assumed* that he was a professional burglar. She finally got out a one-word response: "What?" At that moment, Simon grabbed her arms so she couldn't run away and revealed who he really is. He said,

> "I am a private detective, specializing in stolen works of art, and in tracing, detecting, and exposing forgeries. I'm also an authority on museum security, being a special consultant to principal museums in London, New York, Chicago, Madrid, even Leningrad. I have degrees in the history of art and chemistry and the London University Diploma ~ with distinction ~ in advanced criminology."

Upon hearing all of Simon's credentials, Nicole weakly responds, "You are all that? You're not a burglar?" She asks these questions in tones that reveal immense disappointment on the one hand and shock on the other. She can't believe that he was not what she had thought he was. But even more, she could not believe that he was, in actual fact, so much more than she had thought he was.

When we look at the concepts established by the usage of the terms *salvation* and *save* in the Scriptures, we find ourselves in the same dilemma that Nicole found herself. *It is hard to believe that the terms don't describe what we thought they did, and even harder to believe that they denote so much more than we ever imagined.* Our astonishment creates a natural barrier to the fact that these familiar terms signify a different set of ideas and concepts.

It may come as a surprise to discover that the terms *salvation* and *save* refer to physical deliverances more than anything else. For example, in the OT the term *save* always refers to a physical deliverance from some danger. Not once does it refer to any aspect of spiritual deliverance from sin or from any kind of evil temptation. And in the NT the term *saved* most often refers to physical healing from sickness or from demonic activity.

But neither term ever refers to a salvation from hell accompanied by an assured destination to heaven. If Nicole had addressed this spiritual issue in the movie, she would have asked, "You aren't referring to the free gift of heaven?" in place of asking Simon bewilderedly, "You aren't a burglar?"

It would be hard to accept the fact that salvation and being saved have no reference to hell or to heaven when seemingly everyone has believed it to be so for such a long time. The evidence, it turns out, for both Simon's identity as a burglar and for salvation's referent as a guaranteed place in heaven is nothing more than *a grand spiritual assumption* which happens to be false.

If salvation doesn't refer to the gift of heaven and the escape from hell, what does it refer to in the spiritual realm? Here is a simple list of various salvations with a few of the verses that *explicitly* describe them.

1. Jesus came to *save* the whole world.

> "For God did not send the Son into the world to judge the world, but that **the world should be saved through Him.**" (John 3:17)

> "And if anyone hears My sayings, and does not keep them, I do not judge him; for I did not come to judge the world, but **to save the world.**" (John 12:47)

This is the ultimate or grand salvation that Jesus came to offer and establish. All of the other salvations are connected to it in some way. In this listing of the different salvations found in the Scriptures, we are working backward from the most futuristic salvation to those that save us daily.

What Jesus came to do, He came to do for the whole world. The offer of His salvation is co-extensive with His work on the cross. Nothing would have prevented Him from accomplishing what He came to do *IF* the condition had been met for Him to accomplish His work. Although the condition was not met in the first century, it will be met before He returns in His second advent. Then Jesus will save every single person who has persevered in his belief in Him for nourishment and deliverance from the trials and temptations of daily life. So, a daily salvation from indwelling sin, personal sins, and the temptations of life (while being spiritually nourished by the Jesus) is foundational for a person to experience the future salvation that Jesus offered.

But we must remember this one fact: Jesus never came to save anyone from hell or to give him a free pass to heaven. That ending is a distorted revision of the original script which was written by the divine Author alone. It is surprisingly easy to make parts of the Bible fit into an interpretative framework that distorts the real message of the Bible. But the rest of the Bible was meant to keep us from those errors.

This salvation, planned for the whole world, is *a deliverance into* the coming Messianic Kingdom (from the hands of all those who hate the righteous) that will be established upon Jesus' return to earth.[1] At that time He will ascend His glorious throne[2] and rule the world in righteousness.[3] Obviously, then, this salvation has nothing to do with going to heaven or escaping hell.

2. Jesus came to *save* those who believe in Him *from* the coming Tribulation. 1Thess. 5:9-10

This aspect of salvation is an *unconditional* blessing promised to all who have believed in Jesus as the Messiah. As a result, this

---

[1] Lk. 1:71-75 and Matt. 13:41-43, Lk. 19:11-27 respectively.
[2] Matt. 25:31.
[3] Matt. 4:8-9; Isa. 2:1-4; 9:7; 11:1-5; etc.

deliverance is not brought about because of how God's people may be responding. Persons behaving righteously and persons behaving unrighteously are all taken up together into heaven. This removal occurs as the first seal judgment is unleashed upon the inhabitants of the earth. *This unconditional salvation involves God's promise to save a particular people from a specific trial.*

The people who will be saved are those who had believed that Jesus was and always remains to be God's promised Messiah who fulfills all the roles and all of the promises connected to the Messiah in the OT Scriptures. The specific trial from which these people will be saved is the seven-year devastation caused by the wickedness of mankind.[1] God responds to this wickedness with an outpouring of His wrath[2] that immediately precedes Jesus' return to earth by seven literal years. There will be no time in history that can be compared to this time of rampant wickedness.[3] The devastation is so widespread and the wickedness of man's rule over the nations will be so cruel that three-fourths of all those living upon the earth will be killed during these seven years of chaos. From all this God will save those who had believed that Jesus is God's promised Messiah.

The next three salvations are so closely interrelated that it is difficult to distinguish between them. It is possible that they shouldn't be distinguished. *They could be discussed together as one salvation that varies based upon its opponent.* It has long been taught that man's three basic opponents are the world, the flesh, and the Devil. These next three salvations basically follow that classic formulation. One salvation or deliverance is from this perverse and wicked world. A second salvation is from indwell-

---

[1] Matt. 24:4-12; Rev. 6:1-11; 9:20-21.
[2] Rev. 6:14-17
[3] Matt. 24:21.

ing sin (also known as the flesh). The third salvation, closely related to the previous two salvations in different ways, is from the personal sins that have led man away from the God he loves. In short, all three of the next salvations have to do with walking righteously before the Lord while presently buffeted by the world, the flesh, and the Devil.

3. Jesus came to *save* those who believe in Him *from this perverse generation*.

"Be saved from this perverse generation!" (Acts 2:40)

"... [the Lord Jesus Christ] who gave Himself for our sins that He might deliver us out of this *present evil age,* according to the will of our God and Father ...." (Gal. 1:4)

The reception of the gift of the Holy Spirit, as an element of the message preached by Jesus' apostles, is first set before us in Acts 2:38-40. To walk *perversely* is to walk *crookedly.* When morality or spirituality are part of the context, the term takes on the meaning of *bending the standard,* or of *winding about* instead of walking in a straight line. From the Greek term "skolios" translated perverse, we get the English word scoliosis, which describes a lateral curvature of the spine.

Interestingly enough, *A Manual Greek Lexicon of the New Testament* by G. Abbott-Smith suggests "orthos" which means straight, as an opposite to the concept of "skolios" Walking the way we ought to walk, which may be called walking *orthopedically,* comes from the ministry of the Spirit of God in our lives. So, it is no surprise that in a context that warns the reader about being perverse in his lifestyle, the Holy Spirit is designated as a gift from God to correct such a crooked walk.

Notice how Luke, under the inspiration of the Holy Spirit connects the gift of the Holy Spirit to escaping a bent and crooked world:

"[to the Jews who were responding to God in attending the Passover Feast, Peter said] . . . Repent . . . be baptized . . . and **you shall receive the gift of the Holy Spirit.** . . . And with many other words he solemnly testified and kept on exhorting them, saying, *'Be saved from this perverse generation.'"* (Acts 2:38, 40)

The salvation that Peter offered the multitude depended upon the reception of the Holy Spirit. He would work within the soul of the trusting person to enable him to turn away from all the temptations arising from the world to walk perversely.

4. Jesus also gave the gift of the Holy Spirit in order to save man from something inside of himself. That something is *a part* of his human nature and is called indwelling sin.

This is not the same thing as the last point. In the last point Jesus came to save His people from *an outward enemy*, the world with its crooked perspective and way of life (and from the Devil who rules over the world). In this point Jesus saves from *an internal enemy*, an enemy that we can't get away from because it is *a part* of our human condition or constitution. When indwelling sin reigns as king within the soul of man, it produces all kinds of sins, falling short of the righteousness God desires from us.

Paul explained that the Holy Spirit basically keeps those who are walking by faith in Him *from themselves*. So, he said in Gal. 5:16-17,

> "But I say, *walk by the Spirit*, and you will not carry out the desire of the flesh. For the flesh sets its desire against the Spirit, and the Spirit against the flesh; for these are in opposition to one another, *so that you may not do the things that you please* (or wish to do)."

To walk by the Spirit of God is to obey the leading that He gives by the power and virtue He infuses as a person trusts Him for them. In short, *the Holy Spirit infuses the believing person with the life Jesus promised to give him so that he could spiritually overcome all the trials and temptations he faces in life*. All the time that this is occurring, the flesh is continuing its opposition to the Holy Spirit's leading, either by direct rebellion as here in Gal. 5:16-26 or by insidious deception as in Rom. 7:7-25. The Holy Spirit's ministry within the heart of the trusting individual manifests the freedom over indwelling sin that was once-for-all won by Christ on the cross. Indwelling sin, while it remains a part of man's constitution as long as he lives a physical life, no longer has to dominate his heart, creating death and sin within. This is listed under the salvations that Jesus offers because each time a person is saved from indwelling sin, he has chosen to follow the Good Shepherd, experiencing everything He provides for life and godliness. The other reason that deliverance from indwelling sin moment by moment is referred to as a salvation is that the fifth salvation, listed next, cannot be accomplished without it.

5. Jesus came to *save* them *from their sins*; He saves those who already believe in God and are, with considerable failure, already following Him.

> "And she will bear a Son; and you shall call His name Jesus, for it is **He who will save His people from their sins**." (Matt. 1:21)

Jesus came to save those who have not learned, or have not been disciplined enough, to continually trust in God to overcome the sins in their personal lives. This goes far beyond any initial trust in God or in Jesus for the salvation *imagined* in our theological standards, namely, the gift from God of a place in heaven. The trust that is now being discussed is one that is repetitive; it must take place constantly throughout the rest of a person's life. This trust is for a salvation from the sins that indwells sin (the opponent discussed in #4 above) produces. No one can be saved from his personal sins until he learns how to apply the salvation (or freedom) that the cross accomplished for him from indwelling sin that produces his personal sins.

To save us from our sins, Jesus had to save (or free us) from indwelling sin, the source and cause of all the sins. He did that once for all through His death on the cross. The cross *unconditionally* breaks the power of indwelling sin within. As a result, all men everywhere have been delivered from the necessity of obeying or following that **part** of their constitution (called indwelling sin). They are free to choose their master: either indwelling sin or the Holy Spirit whose job it is to give to the trusting person what Jesus had promised him.

As an enticement to the first century believers in God to believe in Him as the promised Messiah, Jesus gave something called *eternal life.* This life would be different from anything that they had ever experienced in their walk with God; it was, in fact, a taste of the promised kingdom that Jesus was offering even before it would be set up for Israel and the world to enjoy.

So, eternal life is unrelated to heaven or to getting a person to heaven. It certainly isn't a promise of heaven. *Eternal life is the actual life of Jesus,* the one that He lived by or manifested during His life on earth. It is also a foretaste of the life that will be experienced in the kingdom when it is finally set up. And that is all that eternal life is. It has nothing to do with eternity or with being with God forever. When a Christian lives by that same life, he experiences the same victory over temptation that Jesus did. He, therefore, has no excuse for continuing in any sin regardless of its power or attractiveness.

This life is "eternal" in the sense that it is for *this present **age** regardless of how long it lasts.* The term eternal (aionias) comes from the term for age (aion), designating a period of time and is properly translated in most contexts as *everlasting* (i.e., long lasting) or *forever* (having no *temporal* end or cessation *in sight*). His life may become our only nature after we die. But we must not forget what the apostle John said in his first letter. In that letter he expressed his wonderment over the possibility that life after death may be extraordinarily and supremely different, maybe even from eternal life itself. After experiencing Jesus' life (i.e., eternal life) for nearly fifty years, it is hard to believe that there could be anything better. But if there is, it will be the most extraordinary life one can imagine.

Chapter 5

Salvation is by Grace through Faith, but . . .

My brother-in-law has a saying he likes to use to describe any attempt to get from point A to point B when there isn't sufficient means to do so. It doesn't matter if the issue is a journey by car or an intellectual argument. So, when we had visited him and his family in San Francisco, and we were sight-seeing, wanting to see some popular landmark, he would say, "Well, you can't get there from here." That meant that we would have to take a circuitous route to get to a bridge to cross the bay. But there was *no direct way* to get there; there was *no clear-cut, straight path* to the goal being sought. When talking politics, physics, or almost any other subject, the same phrase would be inserted into the conversation as a challenge when the argument that was being used was not going to establish the point being sought.

"You can't get there from here" describes equally well some of the theological sound bites that we have accepted over the years. Taking isolated verses out of their context and making them stand alone as a proof text *supposedly* verifying the view that we are attempting to propagate, we make it known to all studious observers that "we can't get there from here."

Or when we take concepts described in the Bible and relate them in ways that the Bible never specifically does, we actually declare to all listening that we are having trouble "getting there" ~ establishing the theological belief we want to affirm ~ "from

49

here" ~ using the proof text as our short-cut to arrive at our *pre-conceived* theological destination.

This approach to teaching the Bible has plagued Christianity for at least five hundred years. As a result, the opposing views on most issues can't be reconciled because neither side has seen the bigger picture in the battle of perspectives. So, we have Calvinism versus Arminianism, and Catholicism versus Protestantism, and Lordship Salvation versus Free Grace, and Eternal Security versus Eternal Insecurity, and Limited Atonement (i.e., Christ died for some in a special way) versus Unlimited Atonement (Christ died for all in the same "special" way), and so on. Has anyone noticed that none of these theological positions are any closer to winning the battle that it is fighting than when it first began? Why is that, do you think?

What if all of these positions are partly correct and partly wrong? *What if* each has its good points, and each has its bad points? Is it not clear that in each case one propagandist focuses upon what is wrong with the opposing view, and, possibly, supposes that nothing exists in that opposing view that is worth the trouble of sifting through all of its points to obtain?

These debates continue to be endless because, in point of fact, both opposing views are wrong in significant places. But neither propagandist thinks it is necessary to set aside his whole view because of what may appear to be some weaknesses in his position. He is certain that his view has, on the whole, captured the essence of the Bible's teachings. But has it?

Now if the reader has received the message of the last chapter, then the next statement will be taken as a necessary application of the point made there. There is a theological debate being waged today (as it has been for hundreds of years). In that debate one side, called Lordship Salvation, says that works are necessarily needed for a *final* salvation (or a *final* justification). This side points to such passages as Matt. 24:13 to defend its view. That verse says,

> "But the one who endures (or perseveres) to the end, he shall be saved."

This passage, as well as many others that could be marshaled in the defense of this view, clearly includes perseverance as a condition for salvation, and perseverance, by anyone's definition, necessarily involves works. Hence, the proponents of this view feel confident that their position, which requires works to be finally saved (or finally justified), is the correct view in spite of verses that don't seem to fit very well with it.

The Free Grace position would charge that this view ignores the immediate context, and, therefore, misrepresents the concept of salvation. And it is a fact that the Lordship position does both of these things. The context is not about some spiritual salvation that gets a person to heaven while he escapes hell. It is about physical deliverance at the end of the tribulation. Consequently, to make the obtainment of spiritual salvation (i.e., the *supposed* attainment of heaven) conditioned on the good works of perseverance is to misrepresent the doctrine.

The Free Grace position teaches that salvation is by grace through faith and is *not related to works in any way*. A classic passage, Eph. 2:8-9, well known by most Christians, is relied upon to justify this view of salvation. Those verses say,

> "For by grace you have been saved through faith; and that *not of yourselves*, it is the gift of God; *not as a result of works*, that no one should boast." (emphases mine)

The Lordship view of salvation dismisses these verses by a semantic play on words. While salvation, they say, does not result *from* works, nevertheless, it necessarily results *in* works as verse ten clearly says. And everyone agrees that this *should be* the case. So, having dodged the apparent restrictiveness of Eph. 2:8-9, the proponents of the Lordship view point to other verses and concepts that demand, at least in their thinking, good works from the believer for him to be finally saved (or finally justified). If these good works are not present, the greatest probability is the person in view has not been truly saved.

So back and forth the debate continues. While both sides believe good works are necessary and required by God from the believer, they differ on the reason that they are required. The Lordship view believes that the good works are necessary to get to heaven. The Free Grace view believes they are necessary to qualify for service in the coming Messianic kingdom, but have nothing to do with getting a person to heaven.

The debate is greatly complicated by the torrent of circuitous arguments that supposedly demonstrate that these formulations were indeed in the minds of the NT writers. As the average Christian is drowning in the raging, swirling currents of convoluted thinking, it is a rare occurrence that one of them has the circumspection to ask, "Is there a direct statement of Scripture that actually says what you are suggesting by all of your deductive reasoning?" And that is a legitimate question! Do we have to take our stand on layer upon layer of *presumptions*?

But the debate itself can come to an abrupt and lasting end if we understand that the salvation that is in view, not only in the two passages discussed above but in all the passages throughout the Bible, has nothing to do with going to heaven and escaping hell when we die. If that grand assumption can be overruled once and for all, our discussions on Biblical topics would open up and take on an entirely different ambiance. *The theological war between Lordship Salvation and Free Grace turns out to be a moot debate if salvation has nothing to do with going to heaven.* Both viewpoints contain some truth and some error in their doctrinal formulations. That is the reason that neither side has been able to win the debate. Neither side represents what the Bible is trying to set forth.

Some salvations are by grace through faith apart from works, and some of them are by grace through faith with works. The Biblical concept of salvation is too broad to reduce to one simple formulation. As the last chapter tried to explain, there are at least five very different salvations described in the Bible. But you will recall none of those salvations involved the giving of eternal life *initially* or entering the kingdom of heaven *summarily*. Nevertheless, in my own inconsistency, I continued to *assume* that believing in Jesus resulted in an immediate salvation from hell to heaven even though I had already discovered that neither phrase, eternal life nor the kingdom of heaven, was related to going to heaven and missing hell.

Why did I continue to assume that *initially* believing in Jesus saved a person from hell? I was letting the accepted interpretation of two passages, Acts 16:30-31 and Eph. 2:8-9, which were basic to the old paradigm, continue to influence me incorrectly. They have been taken to convey the idea that a salvation takes place at initial faith. Even though I have come to learn through detailed word studies that no reference to salvation meant the obtainment of heaven, I had not specifically related that truth to these two passages. Consequently, I naturally assumed what the old paradigm had taught me, namely, that the reception of eternal life at the moment Jesus was believed in was a salvation (from hell with a guarantee of heaven). But since such an idea is nowhere *explicitly* declared to be so, I have come to a better, more consistent understanding of those two passages.

Eternal life, given for the new birth, is granted for the purpose of equipping the person who receives it to carry out the good works that God the Father has ordained that he should perform. It is given at the time a person first trusts in Jesus. Yet, the gift is given to be used for the rest of the person's life. It is, after all, a *life* that is given. With this life, he can experience a "shared life together" with Jesus in order to be in constant communication with God the Father in all of his obedience.

Because salvation is not about heaven in any way, both Lordship Salvation and Free Grace Salvation are inadequate to explain the doctrine of salvation. But because the salvation that is being debated involves the perseverance of the recipient of the gift of life in good works, the Lordship position is closer to the truth than the Free Grace position is. But unfortunately, when the Lordship position takes the scenario further, requiring the good works *to get to heaven*, it too fails to represent the salvation that the Bible is describing.

The dichotomy that we have been taught which pits grace and faith against works when salvation is being discussed is a false dichotomy. Not only is salvation not about going to heaven when a person dies, it is never described as *a state of being* or *a permanent standing before God* in the Bible. Consequently, it is incorrect to talk about a "saved person" as though his future status or standing is established and is now inalterable. Salvation, one that a person can obtain presently, never describes a person in that way. If the good works that God desires a person to perform are carried out, and even done magnificently, heaven is not, thereby, guaranteed. Heaven is simply not part of the salvation plan of God. Salvation is about living righteously now and, thereby, qualifying for kingdom salvation in the future upon planet earth.

We have been taught that salvation is *supposedly* spoken of as a free gift of God's grace received through faith *apart from* any obligatory work. This concept is primarily based upon Eph. 2:8-9. But we have been too hasty in using Eph. 2:9 as though it said the same thing as Rom 3:28. It doesn't.

The term translated (not) as *a result of works* is "ek" in Eph. 2:9. The term translated *apart from* is "choris" in Rom. 3:28. These two prepositions do not indicate the same thing. The idea of εκ is that of something coming out of something else. So it would be properly translated *from*, with the idea of *flowing from* something. Hence, the salvation of which Paul spoke in Eph. 2:8-9 did not flow from works. But there is no denial of works being involved either. *The point is only that the salvation spoken of did not spring from, flow from, result from the works that were surely involved in obtaining the salvation described.*

Why were works involved? Because a living, vital, active faith is always *completed* by good works. Only a dead, idle faith has no works. The faith that Paul mentions in Ephesians two was successful in achieving a salvation so it was neither dead nor idle. It, therefore, must have had works flowing from it, completing it. Consequently, Paul is in total agreement with James on this issue.

In Rom. 3:28 on the other hand, the preposition is χωρις which means *separate from* or *apart from*, carrying the idea of total detachment or complete uninvolvement. That is not the idea of εκ in Eph. 2:8-9, however. Furthermore, it must be remembered that Paul is only denying the need of works of the Mosaic Law for a righteous life to be led. He never said that works were not involved in justification. Consequently, both justification and salvation typically involve works just as both Paul[1] and James *explicitly* said.

---

[1] Rom. 2:13; Acts 13:38-39. This truth is actually the purpose for Paul writing both the book of Romans and the book of Galatians. He is not denying that works are involved. He is denying that works of the Law need to be involved.

Chapter 6

Connecting the Dots Properly

On my first trip to India to train pastors, I used an illustration to assure the pastors that what I was about to teach them would enable them to make the Bible simpler without leaving out any doctrine with which they were familiar. I put five dots on a blackboard and asked the pastors for the name of five doctrines that they wanted to learn more about. Any five doctrines could have been used to illustrate the point I was making. Then I asked the pastors to connect the dots for me.

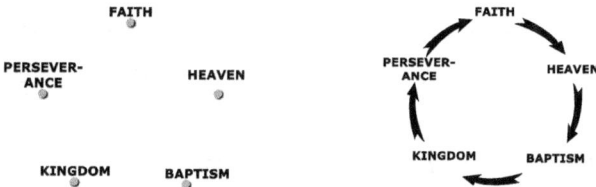

FAITH   FAITH

PERSEVER-   HEAVEN   PERSEVER-   HEAVEN
ANCE   ANCE

KINGDOM   BAPTISM   KINGDOM   BAPTISM

Then I redrew the five dots and relabeled them with the same doctrines as before. But this time I asked the pastors if those same doctrines might take on vastly different meanings if they were connected to each other differently. Then I connected the dots in the manner below.

FAITH   FAITH

PERSEVER-   HEAVEN   PERSEVER-   HEAVEN
ANCE   ANCE

KINGDOM   BAPTISM   KINGDOM   BAPTISM

Then I said, "We should not deny or ignore any of the doctrines the Bible sets before us; but we must connect them to each other properly. The picture we get can be radically different."

So, for example, I should not deny *the doctrine of election*; it is a fact of Scripture. But whether it is connected to the doctrines of salvation or justification, as those doctrines are understood today, is highly questionable.

I should not deny *the doctrine of perseverance*; it is a command of Scripture. But whether it is connected to the doctrines of salvation or justification, as those doctrines are understood today, is highly questionable.

I should not deny *the doctrine of baptism*; it is clearly set forth in the Scriptures. But whether it is connected to the doctrines of salvation or justification, as those doctrines are understood today, is highly questionable.

I should not deny *the doctrine of repentance*; it is clearly a requirement of God for kingdom entrance in the Scriptures. But whether it is connected to the doctrines of salvation or justification, as these doctrines are understood today, is highly questionable.

I should not deny *the need for righteousness* as a condition for kingdom entrance; it is clearly taught in both testaments of Scripture. But whether it is a gift *imputed* (that is, given once for all as a free gift) to the person at the time of his initial belief either in God or in Jesus is highly questionable.

It is *the connection* of these doctrines that is the major issue, not whether they are present in the Scriptures.

As a rule Christians have not developed the discernment that they need to guard themselves against inadequate explanations of the Scriptures. (I suppose many will be asking their spiritual leaders about the teachings suggested in this book.) But if I am representative of the rest of the leaders in Christianity, then I would warn you that they may be lacking the discernment that they need just like you do at times. It took me over thirty years to begin to question some of what I had been taught. It was not easy, and it was certainly no fun, to question the tenets of mainstream Christianity. But God expects us all to be involved in it.

It is not the intent of any of my writing to deny anything that the Bible teaches. I believe it is the highest authority a Christian has. My purpose is to challenge all students of the Scriptures to a more accurate understanding of what the Bible is actually saying. I believe that most of us have followed traditions that are not faithful representations of what the Bible sets before us. I know that I have done this in the past.

Back in the early eighties, I developed a Christmas Quiz for Probe Ministries' radio program. It became the most popular and most asked for radio transcript that they had produced. My intention from the beginning was to have fun. That doesn't sound very spiritual, does it? I wanted to have fun while I went through the back door, so to speak, to suggest that we know our Christmas traditions better than we know our Bibles. But because it wasn't intimidating, lots of Christians had fun with it, even using it for a family devotional during the Advent Season.

But not all Christians were entirely happy with it. Someone very close to me asked me once, "Why do you want to ruin our Christmas traditions?" This person's church Christmas pageant always had the same characters fulfilling the same roles to the joy and delight of everyone present. Well, when I suggested that there were more than three gifts that the wisemen brought, and that there were, most likely, more than three wisemen, and that they didn't get to the baby until he was a one-to-two year old toddler, the traditional Christmas pageant became a rather awkward, if not tense, time each year. It isn't necessarily true that Christians want the truth all the time. Lots of times they would rather have what they are familiar with, especially if it is accompanied by a sense of peace and security, howbeit, an entirely false sense.

That is the reason we need both encouragers and preachers in the Body of Christ. An encourager comforts the afflicted; a preacher afflicts the comforted. Praise God that those spiritual gifts still abound today. We are all commanded to seek the truth through diligent study. Will we be obedient in that pursuit?

Since all the dots need to be connected, and since connecting the dots improperly leads to error in doctrine and to a malaise of emotional confusion, we must take no one's word for how these doctrines fit together. All views must be tested, using the Word of God alone as the supreme authority for what God is saying to us all.

Each chapter that follows will attempt to connect some of the dots that are present in the Scriptures. Since we have no preconceived idea or grid or theology that we are forcing these dots to align with, we can take a fresh look at each topic or subject being addressed and allow the verses in their immediate context to determine what we ought to believe. I hope this study will be enlightening. It certainly was for me. I also hope that it will prepare all of us to better communicate Jesus to a shrinking world that desperately needs Him.

Chapter 7

Salvation and Jesus

When we begin talking about Jesus and salvation, we typically ask the wrong questions. And we do this because we've *assumed* certain things to be true that aren't. I recently read Clark Pinnock's book, *The Wideness of God's Mercy,* and sections of Alister McGrath's two books, *Christian Theology* and *Historical Theology,* along with devotionals written by a popular Christian writer here in Texas. Without going into detail, let me say that *they all assume, rather than demonstrate, that salvation is about going to heaven when we die.* If these scholars take it for granted that salvation is about obtaining heaven before we die, it is not unrealistic to suppose that a great many preachers, teachers, evangelists, and laymen do as well.

What if this ubiquitous *assumption* about salvation is false? *What if* salvation isn't about heaven at all? I suspect that some will respond to these questions with: "Preposterous! Nothing could be more certain than the fact that salvation is specifically about going to heaven when we die."

If that is really true, we ought to be able to cite a lot of verses that can prove that point, right? Oh, I know there are a lot that seem to be close to saying that salvation is about going to heaven. And I'm sure you've heard the cliché: closeness only counts in horseshoes and hand grenades. So, let's not give ideas a pass just because they are close to what we are looking for. If we can't find an idea *explicitly* stated, we ought to reject the suggestion that it is a valid truth revealed by God. It is, rather, a mere speculation formulated by man.

When we equate things because they are similar or *seemingly close* to each other in meaning, we begin forming *assumption* after *assumption* until we've lost sight of the Scriptures completely. If you're reading these books in order, as I hope you are, you already know that the paradigm we've used to understand the Bible is wrong, and decidedly so. The Bible is not about heaven and hell. It is about life on this earth; it is about man fulfilling the purpose for which he was created. That purpose is to represent God in all that he does as he trusts in Him.

Heaven is not the same thing as salvation, or eternal life, or the kingdom of heaven. Hell is not the same thing as perishing, or being condemned, or going to destruction. When all these concepts are properly understood, we realize that they aren't even *close* in meaning to the ideas presented to us in the traditional paradigm that is so familiar to us.

The traditional thinking about Jesus and salvation can be set forth in a few lines of a familiar syllogism:

Believing in Jesus is the only way to obtain salvation.
Salvation is about securing one's place in heaven after death.
Hence, if you don't believe in Jesus, you can't go to heaven.

That summarizes what most of us have been taught. But it does not represent what the Bible actually teaches. Horseshoes and hand grenades this isn't.

As we begin to study these matters on our own, we learn some truths that don't harmonize well with what we've been taught. For example:

No one in the OT *was* ever said to be **spiritually saved**.
No one was described as being **born again**.

No one was given eternal life.
No one was *given* the *Holy Spirit* upon believing in God.

Yet:

Many lived lives that were acceptable to God.[1]
Some were even praised by God.[2]
And these, it is revealed, are in God's presence after they died.[3]
And many lived their lives in the hope of securing a place in the resurrection of the righteous, believing in a judgment by God over their lives.[4]

These *facts* present us with more than a few problems. The OT is filled with people who, if Abraham, Isaac, and Jacob are meant to be representatives of all those who were responding to God in faith, did not know Jesus, were not saved (in the traditional Christian sense of being delivered from hell and given heaven in its place), and yet ended up in the presence of God. If we will allow it to do its job, the OT will teach us that going to heaven is not dependent upon knowing about or believing in Jesus.

It is true that apart from Jesus there is no gift of eternal life. But this gift is never described as an aspect of the initial and instantaneous salvation that is central to Christian theology. And there is so much more to the story than that. The story really takes such drastic turns that it does not come close to the place where most of our current theologies would lead us.

Connecting the dots between Jesus, salvation, eternal life, and heaven is the place to discuss *the doctrine of progressive revelation.* That doctrine simply states the obvious truth that God did not reveal all of His truth in the beginning; He revealed it grad-

---

[1] Heb. 11:1-40, esp. vv. 2, 39.
[2] David in Acts 13:22; Moses in Ex. 33:12-17 and in Deut. 18:18-19; Job in Job 1:8.
[3] Cf., Matt. 22:31-32.
[4] Acts 23:6; 24:14-16, 25.

ually and progressively as history ran its course under His providence. One of the consequences of this obvious truth is that a person is not held accountable for revelation that was not given to him. He is responsible for only what was made known to him.[1] Do you not think that is eminently fair? Would not God be unfair on any other basis? Of course He would.

Since this is true, and for most a self-evident fact, we must not read the NT back into the OT. It is a mistake to *assume* that what became true for later individuals was also true of those who lived before them. *Like any history, or any novel for that matter, the Bible is meant to be read from front to back, allowing the story to unfold naturally.* Characters at the beginning may not know the information that the characters at the end know. And this is exactly what one expects as he reads along.

No one can be justly responsible for believing revelation about Jesus if he had not been given that revelation to believe. So, for example, none of Israel's patriarchs had to believe that the Messiah would be like Moses since that revelation was not given to any of them during their lifetimes.[2] They didn't even know who Moses was much less a Messiah that was supposed to be like him.

In the same way, none of the generations from Moses to the time of the prophet of Isaiah can be justly responsible for knowing the time predicted for the appearing of the Messiah since that revelation was not given until Daniel revealed it in his book of prophecies.[3]

But once God revealed something new, those who were exposed to that information needed to believe it and pass it on to

---

[1] John 15:22-25.
[2] Deut. 18:18.
[3] Dan. 9:24-27.

the generations that followed. Jesus clearly broached *the doctrine of progressive revelation* when He said,

> "But blessed are your eyes, because they see; and your ears, because they hear. For truly I say to you, that many prophets and righteous men desired to see what you see, and did not see it; and to hear what you hear, and did not hear it." (Matt. 13:16-17)

Those who came before missed out on both the revelation that would be revealed to later generations and the experiences that responding properly to the new revelation would bring.

In the NT, the reception of eternal life is an example of this. Eternal life wasn't given until Jesus' earthly ministry. *When it was finally offered, it was given to those who were already responding positively to God.* Jesus came to give this life to those who already belonged to God the Father.[1] He came to save "His people"[2] by giving them this extraordinary life that turns them into supernatural conquerors over all temptations.[3] That fact ought to change the way we look at the whole message of the Bible.

Matthew isn't giving some convoluted statement; he isn't saying that Jesus has come to *save* every single Israelite who had strayed from the divine Shepherd,[4] bringing him back to the Shepherd of man's soul.[5] This *salvation from* personal sins would be accomplished by the Good Shepherd as His life flowed into His sheep *keeping them from* their sins.[6] This is the primary method the Good Shepherd uses today to produce the righteousness that is needed to qualify for entrance into His kingdom experi-

---

[1] John 17:1-2, 6.
[2] Matt. 1:21.
[3] Rom. 8:37.
[4] Cf., Gen. 48:15; Lk. 15:1-7.
[5] 1Pet. 2:25. Cf., John 10.
[6] 1John 3:5-6.

ence.[1] Those who have heard about Jesus, have believed in Him, and continue to response to Him in faith have an advantage over those who have never heard, believed in, and followed Him. That is the reason He is to be proclaimed to the world.

The salvation that Jesus offered *God's people* was something that they didn't already have even though they already belonged to Him.[2] So, whatever the Scriptures tell us that those had who were responsive to God in the OT, the life that Jesus offered was in addition to it. The salvation that they could get didn't change their *status* before God (in fact, the Bible never talks about such a concept as *status* or *standing* before God. Man alone made that concept up.); it didn't grant forgiveness of sins; and it didn't guarantee them any blessing in the afterlife. They already had a relationship with God (not some supposed legal standing before God); forgiveness had already been applied to them; and their lives were already pleasing to Him. They were, after all, already *God's people*!

---

[1] Rom. 6:12-13, 16; 1Pet. 2:24-25.
[2] John 17:2, 6, 9.

Chapter 8

Salvation and the Guarantee of Heaven

College basketball passed a ruling some years ago determining the number of years that a college student had to spend in college before he was eligible for the NBA draft. The powers that be decided that a student only needed to spend one year in college before he could be drafted even though in the sport of football three years was required. That rule became known as the "one-and-done" rule for college basketball players.

In the old, theological paradigm that looked at life as a courtroom scene with a Judge ready to rap His gavel and declare each person either acquitted or guilty, and eternally so, there exists a similar idea to college basketball's one-and-done ruling. We were taught that each person who does this one thing, believe in Jesus, is saved from hell and is guaranteed, or at least becomes eligible for, heaven. Salvation was clearly about getting one's ticket punched for heaven in the old paradigm.

In fact, as I have now come to realize, the desire to secure for ourselves an eternal destiny with God is largely the motivation for accepting one theory of the atonement above all of the others.[1] Only one theory of the atonement ~ an explanation of the reasons for Jesus' death ~ guarantees man a heavenly destiny. That is the theory that most within Christendom accept as the best explanation of Jesus' death. Coincidence?

---

[1] Charles C. Ryrie, *Basic Theology*, Chariot Victory Publishing, pp. 308-09.

Is a guaranteed place in heaven with God part of the promise that Jesus gave to each person who believed in Him? As surprising as it may seem, Jesus *never* promised to give that inheritance to anyone. In fact, that transaction ~ belief in Jesus for a place in heaven ~ *never* arose for discussion throughout His ministry upon the earth. He *never* promised heaven as a result of belief, nor did anyone ever come to Him to seek heaven. To get that message there are lots of dots that need to be connected, dots which the Bible never connects.

Such a message gives us both peace and complete security about the afterlife. And that was such a cherished doctrine that in my own spiritual training I was taught to confidently hurl anathemas toward anyone who even gave the appearance of requiring works as a condition for being *saved* (that is, *for going to heaven*). Obviously, if salvation is about going to heaven and if works are required for the great salvation that Jesus came to insure, then a person might lose heaven simply because his works might not be good enough.

Those with whom I was, and still am, affiliated propagated the doctrine of Free Grace. Basically, that doctrine tried to establish the fact that salvation is a free gift. And because it is, works cannot be involved in its attainment. One's eternal destiny is secured by having faith in Jesus apart from any works at all. But our belief was based upon the *assumptions* that salvation referred to going to heaven and that Paul's explanation of both salvation and justification denied that works were involved. You can easily confirm for yourself with the use of a good concordance that salvation is never about going to heaven and that both justification and salvation require works, typically speaking.

The opponents of the Free Grace position believe that works

are involved in a person going to heaven. Some of these try to disguise their belief that works are required for this heavenly destiny (called salvation). They do this by making works the *necessary results* or *inevitable consequences* of genuine faith. But this simple fact remains: *if the works are not present, the person does not get to heaven according to this view.*

I don't know when the battle first began, but by the time I went into the ministry, the battle lines were clearly drawn, and the fight was in full rage with no end in sight. Are works required for salvation? Some say, "Yes;" others say, "No." But both say it with a lot of intensity and passion because it is such an important battle to win.

What if the battle that is being fought is over a misunderstanding?

What if both sides have missed the message of the Bible?

What if the Bible isn't about going to heaven and missing hell in the first place?

What if both are partly correct and partly wrong?

What if salvation is about living a God-pleasing life now and has nothing to do with securing a heavenly destiny?

I now realize that those who require perseverance from the saints are correct. But the problem is the perseverance that is required has no connection to the doctrine of salvation as it was formerly explained. A person can be saved (i.e., believe in Jesus and *supposedly* be guaranteed a heavenly destiny according to the old paradigm) and not persevere, or he can be unsaved (i.e., not believe in Jesus according to the old paradigm) and persevere. *It is perseverance, not salvation per se, that is connected to the afterlife.* Of course, the new paradigm also understands salvation in a way that connects it to the afterlife as well. Do you see how important it is to connect the dots properly?

The salvation that can be presently obtained is a gift from God and is obtained wholly by grace *through* faith (but that faith is a James two kind of faith). After attaining it just that way, there is no guarantee of heaven and no assurance of missing hell. So, after one has received *this salvation*, he is no closer to heaven than he was before he received it. And he is no further away from hell than he was before he received it. This present salvation is a deliverance from our personal sins and from the temptations of the world, the flesh, and the Devil. This salvation has the potential of occurring as many times as we are tempted to sin. How many times would that be for you in your typical day?

There is a need for perseverance *in* the faith *by* faith for the salvation that is still future. And like the salvation that can be presently obtained, this future salvation is not about heaven or hell. It is about the Messianic Kingdom that only the qualified can enter. A righteous life is the standard for that entrance.

The point in all of this is to clarify and establish once and for all the fact that the debate between Lordship Salvation and Free Grace is useless. Both sides are trying to make a square peg fit into a round hole. Both sides are partially correct and mostly wrong. So, if you think that I am trying to mediate between those two positions, that comment should deter you from supposing I have any such goal in mind. We need to drop that debate entirely and move on. Both sides are working from the same false presuppositions that can't lead them to the truth the Bible is setting forth.

Eternal Security

If salvation is not about the afterlife, that is, if salvation is not about going to heaven when a person dies, then the whole doctrine of eternal security is really meaningless. There is no eternal security because there is no place in heaven being offered by Jesus in the first place. This doctrine logically sprang from the traditional, forensic paradigm that has been placed over the Bible to understand it. If God were a Judge whose verdict is sealed with the rap of His gavel, then a person once freed from the *supposed eternal penalty* on sin is logically freed from that penalty forever. This one verdict settles, the old paradigm tells us, the question of eternal destiny once and for all.

Receiving Jesus, according to this paradigm, has commonly been likened to obtaining fire insurance. Who doesn't want fire insurance? And if it is obtained so simply ~ by one response of faith ~ who in their right mind would turn it down?

In all of this, we turned the Bible upside down. We ought to think through the arguments that we have been taught to prove the doctrine of eternal security. Is any part of it based upon the straightforward statements of Scripture? Or are all the points tortuously circuitous in nature?

As I look back on the reasons I was given for believing in eternal security, I find them unconvincing at best. All of the arguments given for this doctrine are so convoluted that they convince only those who are predisposed to believe the doctrine in the first place. And who isn't so inclined?

Let me give an example of the circuitous reasoning that must be used to establish the doctrine of eternal security. Jesus's interaction with the Samaritan woman at Jacob's well is a good illustration. After offering her "living water," He said,

"... whoever drinks of the water that I shall give him shall never thirst (again); but the water that I shall give him shall become in him a well of water springing up to eternal life." (John 4:14)

While interpretations may vary on the identification of "the water," yet it is generally agreed that since a person's thirst, once quenched, can never reoccur, the need for living water can never reoccur. Logically then, once a person receives the water that Jesus offers, he has eternal life and can never lose it since *he can never become thirsty again*. Even though Jesus' statement contradicts what we experience in everyday life, He is authoritatively describing the spiritual realm. Because of who He is, His assertion must be accepted as truth. As a result, the person who believes in Jesus becomes *eternally saved* or *eternally* secure in his *salvation*.

Traditionally, we have closed the case at this point *assuming* that both salvation and eternal life determine a person's final destiny. But we've already learned that salvation only concerns this earthly life. And since eternal life, being the actual life of Jesus, describes the experience of His life in relationship with God the Father and with Himself, according to John 17:3, Jesus' promise to the Samaritan woman only covers her earthly life and no more.

Jesus explained eternal life fully but concisely in John 10:10b when He said,

"… I came that you might have life and have it abundantly."

The life Jesus offered is nothing less than His very own life to be lived right now. As a result Paul could say,

"I have been crucified with Christ; and it is no longer I who live, but **Christ lives in me**; and the life which I now live in the flesh **I live by faith in the Son of God**, who loved me, and delivered Himself up for me." (Gal. 2:20)

And again, in Eph. 3:16-17, Paul says,

"... that He [God] would grant you, according to the riches of His glory, to be strengthened with power through His Sprit in the inner man; so that *Christ may dwell in your hearts through faith* ...."

When a person lives by the eternal life that is given to him, Christ Himself is the source of all of his responses. This is the reason that no Christian has any excuse for sinning. And to whom much is given, much is required. God expects man to be a good stewardship of the life that He has entrusted to him. It will turn the ordinary into the extraordinary.

If the Bible is not about going to heaven in the first place, how does the idea of being certain that you are going to heaven make sense?

If God is not offering heaven as a free gift, why would there be a need for a doctrine that gives a person certainty that he is going there?

If salvation is about *this life*, we should not find it addressing *the next one* in any way.

The doctrine of eternal security doesn't fit the message of the Bible. It is as simple as that.

Assurance of Salvation

If salvation is not about heaven, then to be sure of one's salvation is not to be sure of making it to heaven after death. Rather, *assurance of salvation is the confidence one has about what he obtained from Jesus when he believed in Him.* So instead of being sure that one ends up in heaven, a person can be sure that he has obtained eternal life because Jesus promised He would give it to whoever believed in Him as the Messiah.[1]

But neither *the doctrine of assurance of salvation* nor the *doctrine*

---

[1] John 6:47; 20:31.

of eternal security lays a foundation for confidence about the place where a person will spend eternity. Since the Bible is not about eternity, how could they?

The Bible is about the privilege of walking with God now. If a person is not interested in availing himself of that privilege now, why should he think that God would be interested in having him in His presence for all eternity without some change in his heart? Grace and faith do not get a person to heaven, but they do provide for the experience of a taste of heaven while upon the earth. But if that meal is not appealing to a person today, we shouldn't expect a reservation to be made for him at the Wedding Supper of the Lamb.

Chapter 9

Salvation or the Condemnation to Hell?

Reverend Boudreaux was the part-time pastor of the local Cajun Baptist Church, and Pastor Thibodeaux was the interim minister of the Covenant Church across the road. They were standing together by the road, pounding into the ground a sign that read:

"Da End is Near! Turn You self around Now befo it's too Late!"

As a car with a New York license plate sped past them, the driver leaned out his window and yelled, "You religious nuts!" But from the curve ahead, the pastors heard screeching tires and a big splash. Boudreaux turned to Thibodeaux and asked,

"Do Ya tink da sign should jus say, 'Bridge Out'?"

Most of our problems arise from a lack of good communication. This is especially true in the Christian religion.

If we suppose that salvation refers to the gift of heaven when a person dies, it naturally follows that the person who does not get that gift ends up in hell. I mean, if there are only two possible destinations in the afterlife, and if salvation secures one destination, then the unsaved person must go to the other destination. That is what we've been taught, right?

But *what if* salvation doesn't refer to going to heaven? In that case condemnation might not refer to going to hell. In fact, if salvation is restricted to the life one lives *before* he dies, then condemnation, being the opposite of salvation, would also be restricted to life upon this earth *before* he dies. This seems even more reasonable in light of the fact that there is no passage in Bible that describes a person as being *condemned to hell*. Neither is there a passage that describes a person as receiving a *condemnation of hell*. Don't you find that interesting? If the Bible doesn't use such language, why do we?

Like the term *salvation*, the term *condemnation* is always used temporally. It is never used in connection with hell. Of course, there are various references to punishment or to discipline in the afterlife, and these should be taken very seriously. But the term condemnation is never used for that. In the same vein, it has been questioned by some whether *the wrath of God* is ever used to describe the experience of people in hell.[1]

It is always best to let the Bible define the terms that we are studying. Some are not content with this approach because the Bible does not give, many times, all the information needed to support the *preconceived theological position* that a person is trying to read into a particular passage or term.

So, for example, while the Bible gives a definition of faith,[2] many refuse to accept that definition because it leaves out important aspects of faith that theologians need to support their preconceived idea that faith is a willful response. For them, faith must involve the will. So, because the will is not mentioned in Heb. 11:1, that definition cannot be complete; it cannot actually be a full definition. Their theology has determined what the Bible must say to be accurate; the Bible is not determining what their theology must say to be true.

---

[1] Zane C. Hodges, *Romans,* deliverance from wrath, Grace Evangelical Society, 2013, pp. 276-79.
[2] Heb. 11:1.

In the same way, the Bible's definition of eternal life[1] (or just "life") is unacceptable because it does not refer to eternity. It is too obvious, some say, that eternal life must be about eternity. If it isn't about eternity, then it has the wrong name.

It is extremely unfortunate that the phrase ζωη αιωνιος was ever translated *eternal* life. It is similar to the faux pas that produced "only begotten" as the proper translation of μονογενης in John 1:18 when the more precise translation would have been "unique" or "one of a kind."

Eternal life is a life that if fitted for a particular *age* in which someone is living, "aionias" coming from the noun "aion" or *age*. This *life* can be lived in the present age and again in the age to come which is called the Messianic Kingdom Age. It is "eternal" in the Greek sense of the term alone. It describes the abundant life that Jesus gives *in this age*, and it will describe the experience of all people in *the kingdom age to come* upon this earth.

But in *the age after that*, which is usually called the eternal state theologically, it may not be descriptive of man's existence at all. To apply the English concept of *eternal* to this term is a major mistake and only misleads those who are struggling to understand it.

For the term condemnation, John chapter three gives us enough parameters to contextually form a definition of the term. In John 3:16-21, the apostle records the end of his commentary on Jesus' likeness to the brazen serpent that Moses lifted up in the wilderness. With that context in mind, John says,

"And this is the *judgment*[2] [i.e., the *condemnation* that is pro-

---

[1] John 17:3.

[2] The word group that is used throughout vv. 17-19 comes from the same root and should be interpreted the same way. The NASB translates all the words by the terms judge or judgment. The NJKV translates the same group of words by the terms condemn

nounced]: the light[1] has come into the world, and men (all mankind) have loved more the darkness than the light *because their deeds were evil*. For everyone who practices worthless [deeds] hates the light and does not come to the light so that his deeds won't be exposed. But the one who performs the truth comes to the light in order that his deeds be manifested that *they are done in (relationship to) God.*" (John 3:19-21, my translation)

Here is what John is saying to his readers: God the Father did not send Jesus into the world in order that He would *condemn* the world. That is, Jesus wasn't sent just to rebuke the world's evil, worthless deeds. Rather, Jesus was sent in order that the world might be *saved* through Him, that is, that the world might be delivered right away from their sinful, worthless deeds.[2]

Both the *saving* and the *condemning* are carried out in this life as the rest of John's comments explain. The one who *is trusting* in Jesus is not *being condemned* while his trust is being exercised. But the one who is not presently trusting in Jesus has been condemned already because he has not begun to (or come to the point of) trust in the name of the unique Son of God in order to bring forth good deeds. The one who *has not begun to trust* in Jesus for deliverance (salvation) from the trial that currently stands before him (like the serpents that crawled into the midst of the Israelites, injecting lethal poison with every bite), *is already condemned* for his present faithless response. Such a response is sure to lead to despair eventually or death somewhere along the path being taken.[3]

And this is the condemnation that can be pronounced at that

---

or condemnation. It is important to keep the consistency of thought of the apostle John and not to suppose there are two different ideas present in the context.

[1] Of course "light" could be capitalized as a reference to Jesus (see John 1:9).

[2] Cf., Matt. 1:21.

[3] Cf., 1Cor. 10:9-10; Rom. 7:14-25.

point: men have loved the darkness more than the light because their deeds were worthless, and they didn't want to repent and choose righteousness over their wickedness. At no point is the condemnation that John says is falling upon the one who is not believing in Jesus a reference to hell. This condemnation is a declaration of the wickedness present in men's deeds and in their intentions.

In other words, *instead of justifying men's present actions, declaring them to be righteous, God is condemning men's present actions, declaring them to be evil.* Now the point not to be missed it this: the condemnation about which John wrote is the flip side to the apostle Paul's concept of justification.[1] And neither has anything to do with a person's eternal destiny.

When we understand the contexts of the terms that are used, and we refuse to allow *preconceived, theological ideas* to sneak into the interpretation, the message of the Bible is radically different from what we have been led to believe. Let's take the classic verse of John 5:24 as an example to demonstrate this difference.

If you are like me, you have been taught that this verse is key for establishing the doctrine of eternal security. But if we allow the context to guide us, we discover that it doesn't broach that issue at all. The point of what is being said ought to be discovered from the context and the words that Jesus used. The context in this cast will require us to go back to chapter three for help. But in John 5:24, the apostle John recorded Jesus as saying:

> "Truly, truly I say to you that the one who hears My word and believes in the One who sent Me has eternal life and into judgment he does not come but rather he has passed out of death into life."

The focus of this verse is upon *what is presently happening* to

---

[1] Relate Rom. 1:17 to 3:24-26 and then to 6:15-16, 18-20 and finally to 8:4.

those who are in the audience that Jesus is addressing. Just like the two options that John described earlier ~ having worthless deeds and hating the light versus having good deeds and desiring to come into the light ~ the two options now are *possessing eternal life experientially* versus *experiencing spiritual death presently*. Spiritual death is experienced whenever there is a failure to believe the message that God is giving.

In other words, if life is being experienced, there is no death and, therefore, no condemnation upon the life being lived. If Jesus' message revealing the Father's word to the world is being rejected, then death is being experienced while God is presently condemning the responses that are being given.

The conclusion that ought to be reached is radically different from the scenario that we have been previously taught. Just as Jesus did not come to offer a place in heaven to the person who believes in Him, He did not come to send anyone to hell because he didn't believe in Him. What He offers is an abundant life to be experienced right now. What He condemns is every response that flows from disbelieving His message that the Father gave Him to communicate. Both *having* eternal life and *incurring* condemnation (or coming into judgment) are repetitive.

Chapter 10

Salvation and Forgiveness

We've been taught by godly men and women who were taught by godly men and women who just happened to use a poorly constructed window or paradigm to look into and interpret the Bible. What is seen through any window approximates reality only to the extent that the windowpane is clear and free of distortion.

Though our old window's workmanship astonished most of us on first encounter, we have been troubled by all the passages that it didn't seem to handle straightforwardly. As we all looked through this window, we imagined that we saw a person, forgiven of all of his sins, all those in his past and all those he is yet to commit. And he received this forgiveness the moment he believed in Jesus. The window that we were looking through told us that a person's sins had been a barrier between himself and an eternal destiny with God. But by believing in Jesus, his sins could be forgiven and his future destiny made sure.

The whole scene observed through that tinted and etched window was a courtroom where people were declared either to be guilty or acquitted. And the judgment of that court was final and everlasting. Since Jesus died to pay the eternal penalty resting upon the sins of the whole world, whoever believed in Him could be forgiven once-and-for-all. Otherwise, the wrath of God would be poured out upon the unforgiven man for all eternity as he endured the punishment that his sins rightly deserved.

81

If that were the message of the Bible, it would be so simple. But not surprisingly many suspect that there is more to the story than that. So, some argue that if a person isn't obedient to God, he will not make it to heaven after all. The forgiveness that he received when he believed in Jesus either needs to be supported by subsequent obedience or more forgiveness is needed as he continues to sin and fall short.

That forgiveness is available, of course, but it is obtained only through repentance and a renewed walk with God. If it isn't obtained, what he had, or what he *thought* he had, depending on the various theological traditions being applied to him, is all lost forever.

In this way, the simple message of the Bible, that one thinks he sees as he peers through the stained-glass windows of his particular church, admits that while believing in Jesus for the forgiveness of his sins is important, more is actually needed than this forgiveness of sins. One could be forgiven today (or at least *suppose* that he had been forgiven), but be eternally lost tomorrow.

Now there is a very small group of Christians who counter this view of the Bible's message. They affirm that if the forgiveness of sins is obtained through faith in Jesus, then nothing more is ever needed to obtain entrance into heaven. They believe that the obtainment of heaven (salvation) is a free gift, and that free gift is separate from any works at any time for any reason. A more comforting message cannot be imagined, nor one more diametrically opposed to the previous message.

Before you pick sides, there are a few disconcerting facts that should guide your decision-making. And these facts only represent the kind of truths that must lay the foundation for renewed thinking on the issue of forgiveness.

> Forgiveness is *never* mentioned in the apostle John's *evangelistic* gospel in connection to being saved or as a condition for salvation.
>
> Forgiveness is mentioned *once* in Romans, supposedly the most detailed message on salvation/justification in the Scriptures.
>
> Forgiveness is *never* related to a person's *initial faith*.
>
> Forgiveness is *never* related to heaven or to hell.
>
> Forgiveness is *never* said to be the once-for-all removal of sin, securing a *permanent status* or *standing* of eternal acceptance by God.
>
> Forgiveness, *typically*, is not related to justification at all as Abraham's *two* justifications *explicitly* verify.

Why are all these points, and there are more, important? They ought to give a person pause as he thinks about the issue of forgiveness. For example, if John's Gospel is *evangelistic*, as most Christians believe, why is forgiveness never related to salvation in his book?

In the same vein, Paul sets before us the classic passage on justification in Rom. 3:21–4:25. But he describes the forgiveness that *may be* involved in it as the forgiveness that is experienced in *walking* with God. This being the case, one wonders how Paul's understanding of justification fits the traditional, legal portrayal of justification handed down to us from Augustine through Anselm and the Reformers. In short, it simply doesn't.

Justification, as I have already shown in the previous two volumes in this series, is an aspect of sanctification, and it *never* describes an initial reliance upon God for forgiveness. In other words, believing in Jesus was never supposed to result in forgiveness in the first place! It can involve forgiveness if the person now believing in Jesus had initially rejected Him. So the sins being forgiven are those related to his initial rejection of Jesus. This forgiveness does not reach beyond that one sin (and how it might have been exacerbated by related sins focused upon continuing to reject Jesus).

Or if a person had strayed from God and is returning to Him as he now begins to trust in Jesus, the sins committed in his wandering ways will be forgiven because he is returning to God against whom his sins were committed. But believing in Jesus does not obtain forgiveness for those sins.

If there is no *initial point of faith* described in the Scriptures, and there isn't, then the old paradigm, regardless of how much it might have made sense to us, is way off the mark. Because if no one is expressing initial faith, then no one is moving from a guilty, condemned status to an acquitted, forgiven standing. And honestly, if I had not been taught that the Bible's message described a courtroom scene between a holy and righteous Judge (God) and a guilty and condemned sinner (me), I would never have come to that conclusion through my own reading of the Scriptures. And I don't think most Christians would have either.

The forgiveness that every person needs is one that makes fellowship with God possible. But forgiveness does not have anything to do with his eternal destiny. This is the reason that forgiveness is never related to going to heaven or to escaping hell in the Scriptures. Forgiveness doesn't extend beyond the grave. The forgiveness obtained in this life will not help a person in the afterlife at the Judgment Seat of God.

It is not difficult to recall several passages that deal with the need of forgiveness for those who have already believed in God or in Jesus. If I've already been forgiven for all of the sins that I'll ever commit, why is there a need to seek forgiveness after I've believed in Jesus?

Back when I was just starting out in the ministry, this thorny little problem caused some concern among the folks with whom I worked. Being new to ministry, I was totally clueless. I simply accepted the final decision that others more experienced and mature than I handed down to the rest of us. At the time I actually never understood the problem. All I knew was this: Jesus provided all that I needed, and I had Him so all was fine.

The old paradigm has a problem explaining forgiveness. The problem itself is created by the theology of forgiveness that man has formulated. You see, we are supposed to be forgiven for all of our sins, past, present and future (yes, even those we haven't committed yet!) at the moment of initial faith in God or in Jesus. This type of comprehensive forgiveness is needed to support the idea that an assured salvation from hell and a place in heaven is possible.

But then the thorny part of the problem arises. If a person has already been forgiven of all of his future sins at the moment of his initial faith, why does he need to seek *repeated forgiveness* for those *same sins* when he actually commits them? The answer that was offered suggested that there are two problems with every sin: 1.) they all, it is *assumed*, carry an eternal penalty requiring an eternal experience of hell; and 2.) they all separate a person from fellowship with God. The *assumption* that there is an eternal penalty resting upon every sin is **never explicitly** affirmed in the Scriptures. While sins do separate us from fellowship with God, they don't assign us to an eternity in hell. The reader should find that interesting.

Forgiveness, all of it, is about this life; it is not about the possibility of obtaining a future life in heaven. Every reference to forgiveness deals with the reestablishing of fellowship with God. That is the message of the Bible; and that must become our message too. To need forgiveness and not to seek it is to invite God's discipline upon us. That is truly a foolish thing to do.

Lastly, we ought to take a quick look at 2Sam. 12:1-23 where the story of David and Bathsheba is recorded for us. Initially David tried to cover up his sin, but Nathan the prophet was sent by God to let David know that God knew what he had done and was about to judge him for it. After Nathan disclosed to David the judgments that he must face for his sins, David confesses his sin openly. Then Nathan gave this revelation about the connection between forgiveness and the consequences or judgments that would normally be expected for the sins one commits:

> "...'The Lord also *has taken away your sin;* (and so) you shall not die. However, because by this deed you have given occasion to the enemies of the Lord to blaspheme, the child also that is born to you (and Bathsheba) *shall surely die.'* ... Then *the Lord struck the child* that Uriah's widow bore to David ...." (2Sam. 12:13-14, 15)

It is very important to observe that David was forgiven by God, and yet part of the consequence or judgment upon his sin remained for him to bear even though his sin had been forgiven. Forgiveness seems to have precious little to do with remaining culpable for the consequences that may be brought upon a person for the sins he has committed.

If forgiveness of sins doesn't guarantee in this life the avoidance of the consequences of the sins committed, how can we be sure that it does in the afterlife? Can a distinction be made between temporal consequences and eternal consequences? I don't think so. Are consequences from sinning the same thing as the penalties levied upon sin? I think so. Therefore, if forgiveness doesn't release someone from the consequences of his sins in this life, then it follows that forgiveness may not release someone from the consequences of his sins after he dies.

If, however, forgiveness has nothing to do with the afterlife, then it is difficult to understand how forgiveness guarantees the removal of eternal consequences. Forgiveness simply has nothing to do with going to heaven or hell. An unforgiven man (i.e., one who, according to the old paradigm, does not believe in Jesus) can go to heaven and a forgiven man (i.e., one who, according to the old paradigm, believes in Jesus) may still go to hell. The traditional idea *assumes* that forgiveness is tied to believing in Jesus. But if forgiveness does not necessarily remove the eternal consequences that are assumed to rest upon every sin, then what does it really matter if someone believes on Jesus or not?

But the point that must be grasped here is that salvation is simply not about seeking or obtaining forgiveness. God can forgive men and still be righteous because Jesus died on the cross to make divine forgiveness possible. God has been forgiving people ever since Adam and Eve's first sin, and He has been doing that based upon the death Jesus would die.[1] *The work of the cross was already being applied to man before anyone believed in or even understood anything about a coming Messiah.* The first prophecies about the coming Messiah vaguely described Him as a person who would conquer Satan who had brought such distress upon the world and upon man through his evil temptations. But there was no revelation, as far as we know from the Bible, over the first one thousand years of human history that the Messiah would need to deal with the problem of sin.

---

[1] Rom. 3:25-26.

When sins began to be dealt with, they were dealt with by animal sacrifice. That method of approach to God actually creates a problem for us. Although the blood of bulls and goats could never take away sin, God still required those sacrifices in order to obtain His forgiveness. Later Revelation tells us that the efficacy of the cross was the only thing that could actually remove (forgive) the sins man was committing because only that sacrifice met God's demands.

The work of the cross was being applied to people who knew next to nothing about a coming Messiah. Consequently, sins could be forgiven without knowing about or believing in this coming Messiah. And that forgiveness God was freely applying to all men who desired to pursue Him. After the first sin, rather than becoming the great Prosecutor, God became the wonderful Provider! The Bible is not about a divine Judge out to get people, but about a heavenly Father out to meet His sons' needs!

Chapter 11

Salvation and Righteousness

The story of Cornelius was discussed in volume two of this series entitled *Acceptable to God, without being Saved*, so I won't repeat that information here. But it is important to understand that Cornelius was, as the soldiers that were sent to Peter declared, "a righteous and God-fearing man."[1] And this description was given of him **before** he trusted in Jesus for the salvation that was being offered to him.

These facts ought to lead the open inquirer to ask questions about this scenario because the old theological paradigm has no place for a righteous man who has not believed in Jesus (or who at least has not believed in a coming Messiah). After Jesus came, we are taught, men could be right before God only by believing in Jesus. But here in the case of Cornelius, we have just such a man, *a man who is righteous but who had not yet believed in Jesus.*

What do we do with Cornelius? How do we make him fit into the theological grid that we have been taught? Or is he yet another bit of evidence given to us to show us that the old paradigm doesn't really work?

The easiest response to give is to simply deny that Cornelius' righteousness was *true* righteousness. We could say that it was *legal* and therefore inadequate before God. But that isn't the impression that one gets from the passage, is it? In fact, Peter, we discover, not only went to Cornelius' home to preach Jesus but

---

[1] Acts 10:22.

also to learn a few truths himself. He admitted,

> "'I most certainly understand (now) that God is not one to show partiality, but *in every nation* the man who *fears Him and does what is right,* is *welcome* (or *acceptable*) to Him.'" (Acts 10:34-35, emphases mine)

Peter was putting two and two together. For the first time he understood that Gentiles were *"not unclean."* This is the lesson God taught him from the vision of the sheet coming down from heaven filled with *unclean* animals that he was, nevertheless, told to kill and eat. Now at Cornelius' house he was learning that the Gentiles were actually *"acceptable to God,"* and they were so to the same degree as the Jews were even though they were without the Law and had not believed in Jesus.

And here is the rub. Cornelius, by Peter's own admission, was *acceptable* to God without being *saved* by Jesus. These two matters are not inherently related even though our theological grid of accepted orthodoxy demands that they must be. *Just as Cornelius was, a person today can be acceptable to God without being saved by Jesus.* Peter confirmed this truth for us when he said,

> "... *in every nation the one (anyone)* who fears God and does what is right is acceptable to God." (Acts 10:35, my translation)

Acceptability to God is dependent upon two things: the internal fear of God which manifests itself in outwardly doing what is right before Him. If he *fears God* and if he *does what is right,* with or without the Mosaic Law, with or without Jesus, he is *acceptable* to God. Peter's declaration really doesn't need any further elaboration. It is disturbingly plain. Only a predisposition to reject this clearly stated truth can keep it from dismantling the theology that created the resistant predisposition in the first place. So around and around in circles we must go because the old wine of accepted, familiar orthodoxy is preferred over the new wine of God's disarming truth just as Jesus forewarned.[1]

But Cornelius is not the only one that we meet in the Scriptures who was righteous without believing in a coming Messiah or in Jesus as the promised Messiah. We encounter Job,[2] Noah,[3] Melchizedek,[4] Abraham,[5] and the entire nation[6] ruled by King Abimelech, all of whom were righteous *before* there was a law given by God to man and *apart from* any belief in a coming Messiah. *The Scriptures give no hint that any of these had believed in a coming Messiah as the condition upon which they were described as righteous.*

Part of our confusion arises from the theological dichotomy created by distinguishing a *positional* righteousness from a *practical* righteousness. To this point in my own study, I have concluded that righteousness in the Scriptures is always a practical issue. It always describes a *virtue* that produces a right action or a *right response* in a given situation or it is that *right action or virtue itself.* It is never a *status* that is unchangeable or a *standing* that is permanent before God.

The Scriptures know of no "gift of righteousness" that puts a person beyond the reach of future, divine judgment because all men, those who have believed in Jesus along with the rest of humanity, must stand before God's Judgment Seat. Theologically, that presumed gift of righteousness is referred to as Christ's own righteousness *imputed or given* to a person at his *initial faith* in Jesus. But there is no such gift offered in the Scriptures. *Right-*

---

[1] Cf., Lk. 5:36-39.
[2] Job 1:6.
[3] Gen. 6:9.
[4] Gen. 14:17-18,
[5] Gen. 15:6.
[6] Gen. 20:4 (LXX).

eousness is declared upon the person who, in a given instance, has act-ed rightly or correctly, being obedient to the revelation of God that he possessed. And according to the Scriptures, God never justifies the ungodly or the wicked person.[1] Only our theologies declare that kind of justification a possibility.

In the NT we meet several persons whose righteousness is also indisputably practical. These are Joseph,[2] Mary,[3] Zachariah,[4] Elizabeth,[5] and Saul[6] who becomes the apostle Paul. Not once was the righteousness that these had based upon their faith in the coming Messiah. Rather, it was consistently related to their spiritual walk that was in accordance with the Mosaic Law giv-en to them by God. *Righteousness was achieved whenever a certain kind of lifestyle was lived.*

So, the key thoughts here are these:

Righteousness was never given to the unrighteous;

Righteousness was never *a gift* to the one who was not re-sponding in obedience to God by faith.

Righteousness was never given to turn a sinner into a saint.

Righteousness was never the means of turning an eternally lost and condemned person into an eternally saved and forgiven person (to use the unbiblical terms of the old paradigm that we are so familiar with). Having a perfect righteousness was never the condition that had to be met for a person to go to heaven after he died.

Much of the current portrayal of the Bible's message from

---

[1] Cf., Ex. 23:7 (Although this verse refers to a specific instance of breaking the Mosaic Law, the application must be to all parts of it ~ Js. 2:8-10); Prov. 17:15.
[2] Matt. 1:19.
[3] Lk. 1:28-30, 42-45.
[4] Lk. 1:6.
[5] Ibid.
[6] Phil. 3:6.

the old paradigm is dependent upon righteousness being *a gifted position, status, or standing*. If that is proven to be a falsehood, as I did in the first book of this series, the whole theological paradigm falls to the ground. Thankfully, *Biblical* Christianity is not in the least affected since it is not identical to the Reformed theology passed down to us for the last five hundred years.

Righteousness is never *imputed to* or *reckoned upon* or *declared of* any unrighteous or ungodly person in the Scriptures.[1] *If a righteous response is not given, the declaration of righteousness cannot be pronounced.* Consequently, justification involves responses given by the person who is seeking to do the right thing as he trusts in God who has revealed His will to him. In other words, justification always (well, almost always!) involves good works.

If there is such a thing as a righteous standing or a righteous status described in the Scripture, it is always due to the fact that a person did what pleased God. *But righteousness is never given to or pronounced upon the wicked, the sinful, or the guilty. And this righteousness is never permanent or everlasting.* A permanent righteous status is forever given to the response a person originates, if he is trusting in and responding to God. But no righteous status is ever given to any person forever for any single response he might give (e.g., believing in Jesus). The person may become unrighteous in his very next response just as Peter did before Jesus rebuked him.[2] Yet every righteous deed will be remembered by God forever and rewarded at that person's last judgment.

---

[1] Lk. 18:9-14 can't be used to support the old paradigm because the parable is about arrogant, self-righteousness (Lk. 18:9, 14) and not about a person coming in *initial faith* to God, and because the tax collector obviously already believed in God and was humbly admitting the unrighteousness of his own life. Because the tax collector *did* what God required of him, God could justify *his actions*. No righteous standing was obtained here.
[2] Mk. 8:31-33.

Imputed Righteousness and 2Cor. 5:21

A quick look at 2Cor. 5:21 is required since it is the proof text that supposedly describes a sinner being given (or imputed with) the righteousness of Christ. This is supposed to be the great exchange: Jesus takes our sins, and we are given His righteousness. But is this really the import of Paul's statement? Does this understanding fit the immediate context, the addressees to whom Paul is writing, or the Biblical use of the term reconcile (not to mention the terms reckon [or impute], justification, righteousness, and forgiveness)? As we look briefly at those three issues, the old paradigm will be seen to be woefully inadequate.

The Addressees and the Context

First of all, the addressees must be identified. It seems fairly obvious that the addressees are the Christians in the Corinthian assembly. But is it possible that Paul could be writing *to* them *about* other people? And, of course, the identity of these other people is *presumed* to be, according to the old paradigm, eternally lost and eternally condemned individuals. But that presumption cannot be verified from the Scriptures without the use of the old paradigm.

If one rereads chapters three and four of 2Corinthians, it is quite obvious that Paul is addressing the Corinthians about his ministry among them and how their lives had been changed because of it. *But their behavior has not been a good representation of the change in their beliefs.* The two longest discourses to any church addressed by Paul, First and Second Corinthians, are filled with rebukes and corrections. They were not the only persons in church history who believed in Christ without understanding His full significance relative to walking spiritually. The

94

churches at Rome certainly had the same problem as do the majority of Christians today.

As Paul discussed and compared the OT approach to living pleasingly before the Lord with the NT approach that he and his co-workers experienced, he explained that, while the former way had a glory about it, the latter way has much more. The Corinthians themselves are walking evidence of this truth and a validation of Paul's ministry. If his message about the Spirit's ministry manifesting the glory of Christ in the personal walk was veiled to anyone, it was veiled to those who, for whatever reason, did not believe in the stupendous power of Christ's glory within. But Paul and his co-workers testified to this glorious life through their message and ministry.

The experience of Christ's glory, which is His supernatural life, renews the heart as it makes living spiritually in a trying world possible. Whatever affliction the Christian is called upon to endure, it will be light in comparison to the glory that will be gained by suffering through that affliction according to the will and power of God. Soon we all must stand before the Judgment Seat of Christ to give an account of how we utilized His Spirit and employed His life in our living (deeds). There will be a recompense for both the good deeds and the bad ones. Because this is true, Paul admonished all the Christians in the Corinthian church to have the same perspective that he had, namely,

> "Therefore also we have as our ambition, whether at home [in our physical bodies] or absent [from them], to *be pleasing to Him* [Jesus, the Lord]." (2Cor. 5:9, emphasis and brackets mine)

Consequently, we ought to sustain a certain sobriety about the life-responses we give. They will all be evaluated judicially and righteously, and the person who had given those responses will be assigned a commensurate experience to those responses in the afterlife.

If you think this might be an unnerving and fearful experience, Paul would agree with you. Because this judgment upon each person's deeds will be according to God's righteousness, rather than according to His boundless grace, Paul explained,

> "Therefore *knowing the fear of the Lord*, we persuade men, but we are made manifest to God; and I hope that we are made manifest also in your consciences." (2Cor. 5:11, emphasis mine)

This isn't a judgment to be taken lightly. It won't be an awards ceremony as so many have perceived it. It will be a judgment.

In light of the coming judgment, Paul explained the need to be changed and to live out that change as we give our responses to the situations we face. The change that Paul was urging upon the Corinthians is a thorough one. It begins with a knowledge of our relation to the glorious Christ and manifests His glorious life through us. Paul described the need this way:

> "Therefore if any [man is] in Christ, new creature: the old things passed away and new things have come to be [or exist]." (2Cor. 5:17, my translation)

Paul is not talking about a person being in Christ *positionally* as the preceding five verses affirm. He is describing the way a person lives. Consequently, we ought not recognize each other by the way we have been known to respond, but by the way we now respond or live in Christ. Such living changes our responses, gives us different goals, and provides higher purposes. Living "in Christ" changes everything.

Like the Corinthians, we have lived for ourselves, making decisions based upon what we thought was best for us. Now all men ought to live for "Him who died and rose again on their behalf."[1] By living this way, we indirectly prepare ourselves for the coming judgment.[2]

This was God's commission to Paul; he was given a message to preach. Paul called it a ministry of reconciliation.[3] He was to explain to all people, beginning with the Corinthian church, that God was in Christ reconciling the world to Himself by not counting their sins against them.[4] Because of what God had done through Jesus, every man, beginning with the Corinthians, can come to God and be accepted back into His fellowship and experience His love and forgiveness.[5]

As Ambassadors on behalf of Christ, Paul and his co-workers were preaching this message to all men indiscriminately. Whoever returns to God finds Him standing ready to receive him just as he is. So, Paul begged each man to return to God and be reconciled. God's grace has made it all possible.

God made Jesus in the likeness of sinful flesh and sent Him to die on the cross. By His death He freed each man from sin, the sinful master within his own human constitution.[6] By His resurrection, He offers to man a supernatural life that can not only achieve the righteous requirements of God[7] but experience it in the achieving process. God's righteousness becomes man's only by his *living in Christ* as Paul has explained in verse seventeen.

Rom. 8:3 explains how the sin in man has been overcome through the cross of Christ while 1Pet. 2:24-25 explain the lifestyle that can result if a person lives by the resources given in

---

1 2Cor. 5:9, 15.
2 2Cor. 5:10-11.
3 2Cor. 5:18.
4 2Cor. 5:19-20.
5 2Cor. 5:20—6:2.
6 Rom. 8:3. Cf., also Rom. 6:12-13 and Rom. 7:23.
7 Rom. 8:4-6.

Christ. These are the parallel passages that explain for us what 2Cor. 5:21 really means. Peter says,

> "… He Himself bore our sins in His body on the cross, that we might *die to sin* and *live to righteousness*; for by His wounds you were healed. For *you were continually straying like sheep*, but now *you have returned to the Shepherd and Guardian of your souls.*" (emphases mine)

Christ was made in the likeness of *man's sin* to conquer *man's sin* so that man could be able to live righteously *through Christ* even if he had never heard *of Christ*. God applies certain benefits of the cross universally to all men so that they can pursue Him and receive further benefits from the cross that are conditionally applied. Universally, God has overcome the sin in the flesh; conditionally, He forgives the man who pursues Him. In this way, God loved the whole world. In this way, He has dealt with indwelling sin and forgives the sins man commits whether he has heard of Jesus or not.

God requires His children to live righteously. Man is able to do that because constitutionally the cross has freed him from indwelling sin. That gives every man the ability to respond in faith to God. But in addition to that inward freedom from sin, God gave each person who believes in Jesus a new life administered by none other than His Holy Spirit. And this life, while it is called eternal life in the Scriptures, is the communicable life of Jesus given to man. The reason that the believer in Jesus can live up to God's righteous standard is that he has Jesus' very own life by which he can reach that standard.

To What Does Reconciliation Refer in this Passage?

Finally, the term *reconcile* simply refers to two persons being reunited. They end the conflict between them and restore friendly relations. Sin caused the separation. Either both sinned or one sinned against the other.

But the element that has been lost in the theological discussions of this term is the fact that *it is repeatable*. There aren't many relationships that don't experience *repeated* breaks or fallouts. And every time there is one, reconciliation must be pursued. This is the message of Matt. 5:23-24.

Reconciliation is also repeatable when it describes a person's relationship with God. All the issues are exactly the same. Sin by man follows upon the heels of a broken fellowship with God, temporarily ending their vital experience of life together. Man must in some way acknowledge this as he returns to God. When he does, God stands with open arms, ready to forgive and express His love and care for the child returning to Him. This is portrayed in the Parable of the Prodigal Son, which gives a bird's eye view of the Bible's real storyline.

Paul was given a message of reconciliation to proclaim to all men. In light of the immediate context, the reconciliation that Paul had in mind focused upon repairing one's relationship with God so that it affected the lifestyle a person lived. This reconciliation, then, describes the state of daily harmony that the fear of God ought to motivate a person to sustain with God. It is not a once-for-all state or a permanent status.

There is no reason outside of the pull of traditional theology, which is not sustainable in the present context, to understand verse twenty-one as an example of imputed (a freely given but permanent gift of) righteous. It is not the presence of imputed righteousness that will be judged at the Judgment Seat of Christ. It is not one's presumed standing before God that is the focus of

God's evaluation then. It is the deeds or the works, that one has done as he followed the revelation that God had given to him, that Jesus will judge at the Judgment Seat. If his deeds were done in faith as he attempted to carry out God's will, he will hear the Lord say, "Well done, good and faithful servant!" But no one will be asked whether he had been given a gift of righteousness apart from works of righteousness. Such a gift was not offered by God. Consequently, such a gift won't be searched for by God at the Judgment Seat.

Chapter 12

Salvation and Repentance

A few years ago a movie came out by the name *My Big Fat Greek Wedding*. It was a comedy focusing upon ethnic traditions and expectations. In the opening monologue, a voice, that will become identified with the leading lady's, explained her family's deeply-rooted and dominating Greek heritage. As she gave short character sketches on each member in her family, she explained her father's infatuation with the cleaning solution named Windex. He thought a bottle of Windex could solve just about any problem from cleaning windows to healing cuts, scraps, and even fever blisters. It was the all-purpose anecdote for life.

Repentance is a little like the bottle of Windex in the spiritual realm. Repentance is needed by everyone for almost everything. It is certainly related to salvation. But the question is, "How is it related?" And because there are various kinds of salvation, and since repentance is not related to every one of the salvations, one can easily attach repentance to the wrong salvation. In our attempt to systematize related, but different concepts in the field of soteriology, we have drawn incorrect conclusions because of a failure to distinguish the salvations properly.

Before we can establish the relationship of repentance to salvation, we must see how the Bible connects the dots between repentance and various other issues within the discussion of salvation. These relationships will form for us incontrovertible facts about repentance and give the foundation for the conclusions that we ought to reach.

1. When John the Baptist came onto the scene, he preached a *gospel* of repentance.[1]

    John's *gospel* included baptism, repentance, forgiveness of sins, and good works. As the OT had made plain, and as Jesus would clearly reiterate, a righteous lifestyle was needed to enter the Kingdom of Messiah. For six months there were no other conditions that needed to be met. Nothing else was needed until Jesus, the Messiah, came in person. Then belief in Him became a requirement[2] if the opportunity to believe in Jesus presented itself to a person. Each time a person trusted in Jesus, the gracious blessing of receiving *eternal life* was given. *That life* was God's divine aid to live righteously in this age.

2. When Jesus followed John the Baptist onto the scene, He preached a *gospel* of repentance[3] accompanied by gracious acts.[4]

    In fact, Jesus' message was precisely identical to John the Baptist's as you can see by comparing Matt. 3:2 to Matt. 4:17. And Jesus' gospel didn't change as He moved along toward the end of His ministry as Matt. 4:23, Matt. 9:35, and Matt. 24:13-14 demonstrate. But Jesus adds one thing to His message that is a clarification of sorts to John's message: He introduced Himself as the Messiah about whom John could only say for six months, "He is coming soon after me."

---

[1] Matt. 3:2; Lk. 3:3-18. There are several *gospels* delineated in the Bible.

[2] John 3:3-15; 8:24. The result of *believing* in Jesus was *being born again* which is the same as *obtaining eternal life*. These three issues are interrelated in John 3:3, 5, 15-16.

[3] Matt. 4:17, 23; 9:35. Jesus' *gospel* was identified as *the gospel of the Kingdom*.

[4] Matt. 5:1—7:27.

Being the Messiah sent from God, Jesus preached *a new gospel* that was completely beyond the gospel that John was preaching. Jesus invited His audiences to believe in Him as the Messiah. If they would, He would give them eternal life.

While technically the Bible never uses the phrase the gospel of grace like we do today, grace permeates all of God's good news. But that grace enables the performance of good works rather than being a contrast to them. So, grace provided the gift of eternal life, and faith apart from even the work of repentance laid hold of it. The gospel of repentance was preached relative to entrance into the kingdom of heaven. And grace was offered relative to receiving eternal life. These have been mixed up terribly in the past.

3. The *gospel* Jesus gave His apostles to preach included *repentance*.[1]

When Jesus sent out the apostles two by two to preach in the cities throughout the land of Israel, He gave them a message that included repentance just like His own message did. Both messages addressed the conditions for entering the kingdom of heaven. Since the traditional view of salvation (i.e., going to heaven when a person dies) and the kingdom of heaven cannot be the same thing, the relationship of repentance to salvation must be carefully considered. Repentance is also declared to be the need of God's people, making it impossible to understand it as a condition solely for beginning a relationship with God. Rather, it is the condition for wandering children to come back to the God of their faith so that they can live righteous lives. Practical righteousness

---

[1] Mk. 6:12. Cf., this passage to both Matt. 9:35 and 10:7, and Lk. 10:10-16.

has always been the condition for kingdom establishment and for its entrance.[1] And it was this same kingdom, the one that required practical righteousness, that Jesus was offering. Eternal life appropriated (i.e., drawn upon as one's source for living) was the means to live righteously in order to assure kingdom entrance.

4. The *gospel* Jesus commissioned His apostles and their disciples after them to preach included repentance.[2]

The preaching of this gospel is the Great Commission as described by Luke. None of the traditional passages that are typically labeled Great Commission texts are evangelistic. They are all very clearly describing the discipleship of the world. As Christians go to the world, the message that they ought to be sharing should be explaining how every person can come back to the God who has already revealed Himself to him. God is a loving, forgiving heavenly Father who longs for every creature, made to experience fellowship with Him and to represent Him, to come back to Him to fulfill his purpose in life. Jesus offers all the resources needed to come back to God, to know Him better, and to obey Him in all righteousness.

Repentance is rethinking the decisions that we have made and the paths that we have taken that moved us away from our God. It is God's continuing revelation to us and His conviction of our present state that leads us to begin our rethinking process. The mind *becomes* depraved only when God is finally left out of the thinking process.[3] Depravity, at

---

[1] Matt. 5:20. That righteousness is then explained in Rom. 5:21 –7:12.

[2] Lk. 24:47.

[3] Rom. 1:28.

104

least mental depravity, then, is not an unalterable state. It is like the four soils of Jesus' parable. A person can move from one soil type to another at different times in his life.

5. The *gospel* Jesus gave Paul to preach included *repentance.*[1]

The apostle Paul is very clear about the message he was given to preach. The interesting revelation that Paul gives to us is the apparent fact that repentance is directed toward God the Father while (new) faith is placed in Jesus Christ. If you have gone astray from God, repent and return to Him. If you have rejected the testimony that He has given about Christ Jesus, repent, return to Him, and receive the new revelation that He has given. Repentance is toward God. The old faith is enhanced, not replaced, by the new faith in Jesus Christ, completing the repentance that is needed.

6. *Repentance* and faith are not the same thing.[2]

Repentance and faith must be seen as the two sides of the coin of persuasion. The Book of Acts, in complete harmony with Heb. 11:1, describes faith as a *persuasion,*[3] the result of being *reasoned* with.[4] Later in Acts, the same connection is again explicitly given in these words of Luke who records Paul's interaction with the Jewish leaders in Rome,

> "... and he was explaining to them by solemnly testifying about the kingdom of God, and **trying to persuade them** concerning Jesus, from both the Law of Moses and from the Prophets, from morning until evening. And **some were being persuaded** by the things spoken, but **others would not believe.**" (Acts 28:23-24)

---

[1] Acts 20:21; 26:16-20.
[2] Acts 20:21.
[3] Acts 17:4; 18:4, 13.
[4] Acts 17:2-3, 10-12.

Some were persuaded; others would not believe. Faith, then, is a *persuasion* of the mind or, to use the terminology of the author of Hebrews, a *conviction* of the heart.

Similarly, the Greek word for repentance focuses upon the mind. It basically means *to think after,* or *to have an after-thought,* or *to think again.* Such rethinking *ought* to lead to actions that represent that new thinking. Hence, faith and repentance are similar since they both emphasize the mind or the result of the decision-making process. Faith is simply the reception of God's revelation[1] while repentance is man's rethinking how he left God and His revelation to think his own thoughts and go his own way. Repentance, then, is the renewed thinking that ought to move man back to normal faith. While repentance ought to be a life-long characteristic, it cannot happen at all unless the person is a thoughtful individual who wants to pursue God.

7. *Repentance* isn't the same as the *works* that proceed from it.[2]

John the Baptist came onto the scene in Israel, "preaching a baptism of repentance for the forgiveness of sins."[3] He seems to stop some of those coming out for his baptism to warn them that his baptism of repentance for the forgiveness of sins will not keep them from the coming national destruction if they don't follow up their repentance, baptism, and forgiveness with good works. With this warning, John separates forever repentance from the works that ought to follow it. Lk. 17:3-4 has forever established the truth that repentance doesn't always guarantee a change in behavior even though

---

[1] Rom. 10:17.
[2] Lk. 3:7-18.
[3] Lk. 3:3.

the repentance is genuine. And it is the recognition of this truth that is behind John's warning to the crowds that gathered for his baptism which symbolized their repentance. "Make sure you follow up this baptism with good works that are *worthy* of the repentance that you are claiming to have," he was saying to them. His warning established the possibility that the expected works may not follow the repentance reached.

8. *Repentance* is required of, and can be given by, all men.[1]

God holds all men accountable for repenting whenever they have gone astray. Paul preached it in Acts, and God required it in the Book of Revelation. Because all men can think freely enough, they can both express faith as well as repentance. It is the formation of personal *convictions* or *persuasions* that first pleases God.[2] Then, He continues to be pleased as one walks by the faith thus formed.[3] But having faith and walking by that faith are two different things as everyday life readily confirms to us.

9. *Repentance* is not the need of all men at all times. Faith is.[4]

A man has no need of repentance even though he is still in need of expressing faith. That is another way of saying that man is not always off track. He doesn't always need to be changing his thinking or his behavior in a given area. He can be walking in the light where God is, having fellowship with Him as he walks uprightly. But such a walk is impossible apart from the continuous exercise of faith in the God

---

[1] Lk. Acts 17:30; 26:20; Rev. 9:18-21.
[2] Relate Heb. 11:1 to Heb. 11:6.
[3] Col. 1:9-12.
[4] Lk. 15:7, 10; Matt. 9:13; Heb. 11:6; 2Cor. 5:7.

who is guiding his life.[1] So, while repentance is a response of faith, because both are persuasions, it is not the kind of response that is needed at all times.

10. *Repentance* is required for *entrance* into the kingdom.[2]

This is the message of Jesus, John the Baptist, and Paul. The first message, and the primary point of that message, of both John and Jesus connected repentance to the kingdom. There really is only one way to take this connection if the rest of the truth of the Gospels is mined for the answer. No one enters the kingdom apart from practical righteousness,[3] and practical righteousness is simply doing the will of God.[4] If anyone is not living in this fashion, he needs to repent and began to do the will of God so that he may qualify for entrance. Grace won't get a person into the kingdom of heaven without the good works that flow from it. The contrast of grace to works that we have traditionally accepted is too narrow to explain all of the passages that relate to both. At times grace without works is the point. *At other times grace must be manifested by good works for the grace to be efficacious.*

11. *Repentance* is not inherently about sin since God repents.[5]

Repentance is the Greek term that Jewish translators of the Hebrew Scriptures used to describe their God. He repents, they tell us. When He does so, He is *changing His mind* about a prospective action that He was planning to take. He had planned to bring some level of judgment upon a man or

---

[1] Cf., Heb. 11:6 to Rom. 14:23 and Js. 4:17.

[2] Matt. 3:2; 4:17; 21:30, 32 (but in KJV, vv. 29, 30).

[3] Matt. 5:20.

[4] Matt. 7:21-27. See also the parallel passage in Lk. 6:46-49.

[5] Cf., Jonah 3:9-10; 4:2; Amos 7:3, 6; Joel 2:13, 14; Jer. 18:8, 10. The LXX translates the Hebrew term by μετανοεω.

a nation if those individuals did not repent and turn from their evil actions. Since there is no sin in God for not bringing the forewarned judgment because man heeded His warning and repented, there can be no connection between God's repentance and a wrong doing. That means that the term repentance does not carry any inherent sense of turning from sin.

12. *Repentance* was *never* a condition for receiving eternal life during the ministry of Jesus as the Gospel of John attests.

Throughout the entirety of the Gospel of John, which is almost unanimously understood as the evangelistic gospel, the reader never encounters a single mention of repentance. So, repentance is not a condition for receiving eternal life. For example, a righteous man, such as Nicodemus, having no need of repentance, since he was following God in the fashion God had required to that point in his life, only needed to believe in Jesus in order to obtain eternal life. Being born again was not his responsibility; it was God's since that supernatural act is performed by Him alone. Regeneration occurs as a consequence of one condition being met for receiving eternal life, namely, believing in Jesus. *In this scenario, it can be seen how the use of a phrase such as repentant faith is actually misleading all together*. Faith, simple faith, is the sole condition for receiving eternal life. Repentance is needed only to correct the lack of use of the eternal life that has been received.

Repentance is about returning to God after straying away from Him. It secures nothing beyond this earthly life. Since Jesus never required repentance for receiving eternal life,[1] it cannot be a universal requirement for receiving the resources that Jesus offered to maintain and deepen a person's relationship to God.

God wants every man, woman, and child to change his or her thinking about every issue they ponder. He wants them to bring all of these thoughts into harmony with His revealed mind-set relative to all of these issues.[2] But once a person brings his thought life into conformity with God's perspective in a particular area, there is no more need in that area to repent.

Jeremiah, for example, repeatedly called God's people to repentance.[3] So much is this the case that one might conclude that *repentance is the first step that God's people need to undertake in order to return, or draw closer, to Him.* While it is not the first step for receiving eternal life, it may be the first step in a person's reconciliation after a break has occurred in his communion with his heavenly Father.

These two issues, the reception of eternal life and reconciliation, are not inherently connected to each other. The former is the reception of divine resources for living a spiritual life of righteousness now while the latter is the reconnection to the one, true God through the repentance of man and the forgiveness of God. There was reconciliation present in the OT, but eternal life could not be received until Jesus appeared among His people offering *His life* to them. Hence a person can be drawn to God and can develop a relationship with Him apart from the eternal life that Jesus offered.

---

[1] E.g., John 3:16; 5:24; 6:47; etc.

[2] 2Cor. 10:5.

[3] E.g., see chapters five and eight of the Book of Jeremiah.

110

Chapter 13

Salvation and Baptism

Once there lived in a far away kingdom a young girl named Cinderella. Hers was a very happy life in a very loving family. Then her mother died, and her father remarried. Unfortunately, he chose to marry a woman who had two daughters of her own and who naturally preferred them over Cinderella. Their names were Drusilla and Anastasia. Eventually, Cinderella's father also died, leaving her at the mercy of her stepmother who turned her into the family's personal servant, a role that she tried her best to fulfill cheerfully, without complaint or self-pity.

The King of that kingdom decided that it is time for his son, the Prince, to find a suitable wife. So he made plans to host a ball in the castle for all the eligible maidens in the kingdom. But because it was a *fancy-dress* ball, every maiden had to come in her fanciest dress. Since Cinderella had no fancy dress, she would have to make her own.

When the stepsisters discovered Cinderella's fancy dress, they tore it apart on the evening of the ball, leaving her nothing to wear to the royal festivities. At this critical point, in steps her fairy godmother who turns a pumpkin into a grand carriage, the family horse into the horseman driving the carriage, the mice into the horses that pull the carriage, and the family dog into the footman. She also dressed Cinderella in the most beautiful dress imaginable and gave her glass, high-heeled "slippers" to wear (or at least that is the way the movie portrayed them). But she warned Cinderella that she must be home by midnight because the spell would be broken at the stroke of twelve.

Cinderella had a wonderful time at the ball. And she was the clear favorite of the Prince. But as the clock began to strike the countdown to midnight, she remembered the warning her fairy godmother had given. Cinderella rushed out of the ball losing one of her glass slippers in her flight. But she had to leave it behind before the clock struck twelve and the spell came to an end.

Not knowing Cinderella's name, the Prince's only clue to finding her was the glass slipper she left behind. So, he sent his servants throughout the kingdom to find the lady whose foot fit the glass slipper, promising to marry the lady the slipper fit.

The stepmother had Cinderella locked in her room so she was not available to even try on the slipper to see if it fit her. Her daughters tried with all of their might to make the slipper fit. They tugged and pulled the slipper; they crammed their feet into the slipper as hard as they could. But it just didn't fit.

As ridiculous as it may sound, this is the way some people approach the Scriptures. When they come across a verse that doesn't seem to fit into the theological system to which they are already committed, they try to cram the verse into it. Or they try to *operate* on the verse until enough doubt is created about its meaning or purpose that its import can be sidestepped. The old paradigm made this methodology necessary because salvation, the central pillar of almost all theological systems, was assumed to be about heaven when it is not.

Mk. 16:16-20 is a very difficult passage for all interpreters. For those who believe that water baptism is necessary for salvation (which is *assumed* to be an equivalent to the concept of going to heaven when a person dies), it seems to say exactly that:

no one gets to heaven if he is not baptized in water. For those who don't believe that water baptism has anything to do with obtaining salvation (again, these also *assume* that salvation refers to the free gift of heaven just like the other group does), a lot of gymnastics are employed to make the verse say something directly opposite to what it clearly seems to say: namely, that water baptism is involved in obtaining this salvation.

So, the proponents of water baptism clearly seem to win this argument, right? Absolutely! Well, maybe not.

It means exactly what it says: *baptism is necessary for salvation.* But what salvation is Mark describing? And we must remember that a very strong historical tradition suggests to us that Mark is the scribe of Peter whose *gospel* he is basically recording for the Roman assemblies. Since this is Peter's message that Mark is recording, we should ask the question, "Does Peter give us any information on the subject of water baptism that might help us understand this passage in Mark?" Yes, in point of fact, he does.

Peter addressed the doctrine of water baptism in his first letter. There he told his readers that baptism was capable of saving the person who partook of it. His message there is quite similar to what he said through Mark. He said,

> "And corresponding to that, *baptism now saves you* – not the removal of dirt from the flesh, but *an appeal to God for a good conscience – through the resurrection of Jesus Christ ...*" (1Pet. 3:21)

While there are obvious similarities between the two passages, this one becomes troubling for all interpreters because it seems to say too much. It says, "Baptism now saves you!" I don't know anyone who would make that statement without a lot of caveats. But both passages have at least three things in common: 1.) they both come from Peter (assuming that our historical tradition is trustworthy); 2.) they both deal with baptism; and 3.) they both connect salvation to baptism.

Cinderella's slipper is the perfect picture of how many, including myself, have tried to make this passage *fit* their preconceived theological position. We've done everything known to man, tried every maneuver we could think of, and yet, this passage still seems to elude us. It just doesn't seem to fit with what we know about salvation from the theology that has been instilled in us. Those who want to make baptism a condition for salvation (that is, a condition for going to heaven) understand the insurmountable obstacle of Eph. 2:8-9 that plainly tell us that salvation is "not *from* (*out of*) works." So, they start tugging at that slipper to force it onto their theological foot at all costs of conscience.

Salvation may not be *from works*, but it is never *without works*, some suggest. By this clever little move, they hope to convince us that salvation is not *obtained by works*, but it must always *produce good works*. If it doesn't, that person cannot get to heaven. So, the cliché, passed on from Luther for the last five hundred years, says, faith *alone* saves (i.e., faith without any works being involved grants a person his ticket to heaven), but the faith that saves is *never alone* (it must produce *subsequent* works if it is genuine).

Many Christians simply stop thinking when that cliché is marshaled. Few seem to notice that the statement really makes no sense. In fact, it is a self-contradictory statement as it stands. But it's catchy and cute so many keep it in their theological repertoire to use against all who believe that salvation is offered *apart from* any works at all, those that *precede* faith in Jesus, those that *accompany* faith in Jesus, and those that *follow* faith in Jesus.

114

I want to take the reader through part of the process that helped me decide what these verses mean. We must answer a lot of questions before we can get to the correct conclusions.

First, what was the spiritual state of the apostles being addressed here in this passage?

Second, what is the immediate context of Mark sixteen describing?

Third, what did the apostles believe at this point in their lives?

Fourth, had the apostles already been water baptized?

Fifth, according to the old paradigm, had they apostles already been saved?

Sixth, how does this commission that Jesus places upon them relate to their own needs?

As we answer these questions, we will assume that the conclusions that have been formed in the previous two volumes in this series are true, namely, that salvation, justification, and condemnation describe issues related to *this world* and to *this life* alone, without any direct connection to the afterlife in any way. Because all three of these terms have been badly misunderstood, due to the theological paradigm that they were being forced to fit into, like Cinderella's glass slipper, their true historical meanings have been lost. Let's look back into history and find them.

The Spiritual Condition of the Apostles

There is no one that I've read or had the privilege of interacting with that denies that the apostles were *saved* from hell and guaranteed heaven (as orthodox Christian teaching assumes) at the point when the events of Mark sixteen take place in their lives. They had believed that Jesus was the Messiah sent by the

God of Israel; they had believed His message about His ability to offer and set up the long-awaited Davidic Kingdom promised to the line of David; and they had believed in His promise to give eternal life to anyone who would believe in Him as the Messiah.

It is *assumed* in the old paradigm of historical Christian orthodoxy that believing these points saves a person, guaranteeing him a place in heaven. Since Jesus made it a practice of baptizing His disciples, it is also a near certainty that all twelve of the apostles had been baptized.[1] While many more specific details could be mentioned, the pertinent facts may be restated as follows:

> The apostles had believed in Jesus; they had received eternal life.
>
> They could be described as saved individuals (at least according to mainline Christian thinking).
>
> They had been baptized in water, most likely by Jesus Himself.

Consequently, that raises the question, "How could Jesus be offering to save these individuals who were already assumed to be saved by every theological approach within evangelical Christianity?"

The Immediate Context of Mark 16

Mark sixteen centers upon one fact of history, the resurrection of Jesus Christ. Everything else mentioned in this passage revolves around that fact, being related to it in some way. The resurrection itself is recorded in the first eight verses of Mark sixteen. Certain women, Mary Magdalene, Mary (the mother of

---

[1] Cf., John 3:22, 26; 4:1. The Great Commission assures the continuation of Jesus' method.

James), Salome, and several others, were the first to witness the empty tomb[1] and the resurrected Jesus.[2] When the women who had seen Jesus alive went to tell the apostles that Jesus had resurrected because they had seen Him alive themselves, the apostles did not believe them.[3]

Shortly after that, the two men who had encountered Jesus on their way to Emmaus came to affirm that they too had seen and spoken to the resurrected Jesus.[4] But most of the apostles didn't believe them either. John may have been the lone exception, having gone after hearing Mary's testimony to the empty tomb with Peter and having begun to believe in the resurrection at that point.[5] But he apparently remained quiet about it.

Then Jesus Himself appeared to them while they were having dinner. He rebuked (them for) their unbelief and hardness of heart. He told them that they should have believed the witnesses that He had sent to them, both the men and the women.

Then He gave them a commission to preach *this new information*, this new "good news," this *new gospel* to every creature. This gospel is about the resurrection of Jesus, and about that event alone as far as we know since the context doesn't deal with anything else. Was this *the only gospel* that Jesus commanded the apostles to preach? Certainly not.[6] But it was the gospel, the entirety of the good news, that they are being commissioned to preach by Jesus here in this chapter of Mark's Gospel. We must not read into the term *gospel* what may be found in other texts where the term *gospel* is also used.

---

[1] Mk. 16:1-8.
[2] Matt. 28:8-10.
[3] Mk. 16:9-11.
[4] Mk. 16:12-13. Cf., Lk. 24:13-31.
[5] John 20:8.
[6] Cf., e.g., Lk. 24:47; Acts 26:16-20; 1Cor. 15:1-5.

It must be understood and fully appreciated that *this gospel* was not what the *presumably* saved apostles had believed at this point. Not only did they not believe in the resurrection, they were adamantly against Jesus going to the cross to die. Nevertheless, they already were *presumably* saved (according to traditional, Christian theology), and they already possessed eternal life. Except for the *presumption* that they were saved (from hell), the rest of these points are indisputable, *historical* facts.

The Apostles and the New Revelation

It generally escapes the realization of many students of Scripture, as it did my own, that what Jesus was commissioning the apostles to preach, they first had to receive themselves. This was new revelation to them. While it had been presented to them several times in the past, none of the apostles had received it to this point in their lives. They had resisted the idea that Jesus had to die, and, as a result, they did not understand Jesus' predictions of His own resurrection. They were in a fog about these matters. As a result, they were hidden away behind locked doors in an upper room, confused, distraught, and fearful of their powerful enemies who controlled both the religious arena as well as the political power base of that culture.

Apparently, the apostles needed to add to what they already believed so that they could be saved in a way that they had not been already. They had believed that Jesus was the Messiah promised by God in the OT, but now they were required to believe that He had been raised from the dead three days after He had been crucified. Their previous faith in Jesus had *presumably* saved them from hell (but this is a mistaken understanding). No salvation described in the Bible is a deliverance from hell.

This new revelation had to be received *and accompanied by baptism* for the salvation in question to occur. Jesus was requiring them to add the fact of the resurrection to what they already believed. The salvation, that would follow this new belief and the baptism that had to accompany it, would be different from the salvations[1] and the baptisms[2] that they had already experienced. Yes, this is a re-baptism for them.

The apostles had received eternal life from Jesus by believing that He was the Messiah. That state of possessing eternal life is typically (but mistakenly) thought to be synonymous to being saved within evangelicalism today. But now they needed to be saved in an entirely different sense. The new salvation involved receiving the Holy Spirit by believing in the resurrection of Jesus the Messiah. The Holy Spirit could not have been received yet because He had not been sent from heaven yet.

The apostles' salvations and baptisms were successive because the information that they believed was progressively given to them. In the very near future, really about the time of the Jerusalem Council onward, the message about Jesus would include both His death and His resurrection as the Messiah sent from God. When that message was believed, the salvations that occurred separately for a very short period of time would occur together at the same moment. As a result, eternal life and the Holy Spirit would be received together at the moment of belief in Jesus as the promised Messiah who had died and rose again.

At the time described by Mark sixteen, the apostles had eternal life but did not have the Holy Spirit because He was not available to be given to anyone until Jesus had ascended into

---

[1] Matt. 1:21; John 10:9, 27-28.
[2] John 1:28, 35-37; 3:22-23; 4:1-2.

heaven.[1] The giving of the Holy Spirit is directly connected to a baptism and to an informed belief in Jesus' resurrection both here and throughout the book of Acts.[2] The apostles' re-baptism would have been similar to that mentioned in Acts 19:1-7, and would have been undertaken until all of John the Baptist's disciples (and Jesus' disciples who had not been waiting in the upper room) had been reached with the full message about Jesus and His resurrection.

The *belief* mentioned in Mk. 16:16-17 was different from what the apostles had believed to this point. The *baptism* mentioned here is different from the water baptism that the apostles had already undergone at the hands of Jesus. And the *salvation* referred to in Mark's concluding paragraph to His Gospel was not a salvation (from hell) that the apostles *presumably* had already obtained. Jesus expected the apostles to receive these before they preached them to others.

The *disbelief* in Mk. 16:16 was a reference to the apostles' initial unbelief concerning Jesus' resurrection. The *condemnation* was a reference to *Jesus' reproach of the apostles described in the immediate context for their disbelief of the testimonies that Jesus had sent to them concerning His resurrection.* This isn't about hell. It is about receiving new revelation from God.

The Widespread Misuse of Mk. 16

It is not uncommon to find a person basing his *gospel message* on Mk. 16:15-20. There are several problems with that approach. First, the apostles were already saved (from hell according to evangelicalism's concepts of salvation and eternal life) *before* Je-

---

[1] Cf., John 7:37-39; 16:7-11; Acts 1:4-5.
[2] Cf., Acts 2:21-40; 8:4-17; 8:29-38; 10:44-48; 18:24-28; 19:1-7.

sus gave this message to them. The apostles believed in God and in Jesus the Messiah whom God had sent into the world. They possessed eternal life; they were righteous and pleasing to God (with whom they already had a relationship). All this was true *before* they pursued the things Jesus urged upon them here.

Second, salvation, regardless of which salvation one focuses upon in the NT, is never about one's eternal destiny. Salvation is about this life alone. Like justification, salvation has to do with a person's walk with God while he lives his earthly life.

Third, the salvation that was being offered was one that apparently has to do with the reception of the Holy Spirit who would confirm the message they were commanded to preach by signs and wonders performed by their hands. Mark lists some of these signs in the two verses that follow. This concept of the Holy Spirit confirming the message preached about Jesus with signs and wonders is *explicitly* spelled out for us in Heb. 2:3-4.

This is the meaning and import of Mark's comments on the relationship between baptism and salvation. Every believer in Jesus is commanded to be baptized as part of the discipling process. Re-baptism for receiving the Spirit was a temporary obligation God set in place until the gospel about Jesus was complete and those who had believed in Jesus before His resurrection had occurred had been reached. By the end of the book of Acts, between A.D. 62-64, but certainly before A.D. 73, the time of Israel's destruction by the Romans, these things had been done.

Mark 16:15-16 is simply another example of how a verse can be taken out of its context and misused by well-meaning interpreters. Major Christian denominations have been started based upon this passage and that of Acts 2:38. In one sense these interpreters were already set up for failure by those who went before them. When one understands the message of the Bible as an instruction of how to be saved from hell and presumes that every use of the term salvation carries the same meaning, confusion and errant conclusions are bound to occur.

In addition, to misunderstand the importance of the doctrine of progressive revelation and the fact that not all of the promises in the Bible are given to every single person, passages like this present too large of an obstacle for these inadequately instructed students to overcome. Thankfully our God is full of grace, mercy, and forgiveness. He invites all men evermore into His presence, assuring them that if they will come they will find the peace, joy, and happiness for which they long regardless of whether they have understood the Scriptures properly or not. Can He love us more than that?

Chapter 14

Salvation and the Coming Resurrections and Judgments

There are several different judgments and resurrections described in the Scriptures. This has been a confusing issue for several different reasons. There are two major reasons that I would like to mention. One is the adherence to a theological belief concerning the work of Christ on the cross that does not reflect the teaching of Scripture. Let's just call this bad theology.

Basically we've been taught that because Jesus pays the debt in full that was owed to God because of our sins, we cannot be judged negatively at the Judgment Seat of Christ. But Christ's payment for the sins of the world, while it is completely efficacious for spiritual living while on earth, does not directly affect the afterlife in any way. Each man's judgment concerns his faithfulness or the lack thereof in carrying out the stewardships that God had entrusted to him. It is not about his sins per se in this life. This is the reason that Solomon[1] and Paul[2] both warned every man of his coming personal judgment at which he will receive a recompense for every deed he has done in the body, for both the good as well as the worthless or evil. And Paul, we must remember, believed this *after* he had trusted in Jesus and after he had been taught about the benefits of the crucifixion by none other than Jesus Himself.[3]

---

[1] Eccl. 12:13-14.
[2] 2Cor. 5:10.
[3] Acts 24:14-16; Gal. 1:11-12, 15-17.

The second is an assumption that the judgments that are mentioned occur at the various resurrections that are listed in the Bible. *But there is no reason to confine the judgments to the time of the different resurrections.* There is every likelihood that the judgments are required immediately at death[1] even though the resurrections are designated to take place at a later time. In addition, not all judgments even require a resurrection. At least two involve the living who have never died. There are at least seven separate judgments outlined in the Bible associated with the peoples who had been involved in four different resurrections. Consequently, it appears that whenever a particular resurrection takes place, the people involved in that resurrection have already been judged. But the judgments themselves can be distinguished by identifying the time of the judgment, the place of the judgment, and the people who are being judged. These may be listed in summary form as follows:

- The Resurrection and Translation of the Church
- The Resurrection of OT Saints
- The Resurrection of Tribulation Saints
- The Judgment of Gentiles living at the return of Christ
- The Judgment of Jews living at the return of Christ
- The Great White Throne Judgment Resurrection and Judgment
- The Judgment of Satan and his angels

A word or two will be given to explain and differentiate these judgments. But then, the key significance of all these judgments will be discussed. It will not matter if there is one general resurrection and judgment, as some believe, or several, distinguisha-

---

[1] Cf., Heb. 9:27; Lk. 16:19-31.

ble judgments as others believe. The incontrovertible truth that we will uncover will remain unshaken. In light of this incontrovertible fact, the reader will need to rethink his doctrine of salvation. A gift arising from God's grace will not determine a person's experience in the afterlife. *Today is the day of grace. Tomorrow, the afterlife, will be the day of God's justice. Jesus did not die to meet God's justice in the afterlife; He died to offer His grace today.*

The Resurrection and Translation of the Church

The Bible does not indicate that the practically righteous have been separated from the practically wicked at this judgment. *Since there is no such thing as the attainment of a positional righteousness before God that secures a person's eternal destiny, every judgment in the Scriptures is an evaluation of a person's works.* What he did, rather than what he believed or in whom he believed, will be the focus of this judgment. If a person obeyed by faith the revelation God gave him, he will be rewarded. If he did not, he will be judged for not doing what he was created to do. Every creature has the same commission from the God who created him. Some have more revelation than others; some have more benefits than others; but all have the same responsibility.

This judgment is only for those who had the opportunity to believe in Jesus and had done so when they were given that opportunity. It is not for those who have never heard about Jesus or those who had rejected Him when they did hear about Him. Describing a person as a saved individual, as though that description in some way guaranteed a blissful future, is something the Bible never does. In fact, it rarely even identifies a person as a saved (past tense) individual at all. When it does, it is describing his past rescue from his past personal sins.

125

The Bible does not *explicitly* tell us that all believers in Jesus are judged at the same time, nor that the judgment of the Raptured (or translated) believers is accompanied by the judgment of the resurrected believers. The resurrected believers may have been judged the moment they died just as the rich man and Lazarus were when they died.[1] But two things are certain: 1.) both the raptured believers and the resurrected believers are *judged in heaven rather than upon the earth*; and, 2.) there is *a translation of living believers that accompany the resurrection of deceased believers*. And those facts will help distinguish the judgment of the Church from other judgments and resurrections in the Scripture.

The Resurrection of the Tribulation Saints

If the book of Revelation is understood chronologically as it presents itself,[2] then the resurrection of the tribulation saints[3] occurs immediately after the second coming of Jesus the Messiah.[4] Logically this resurrection must take place after the tribulation has been completed but before the millennium begins. It is the *faithful peoples* from the tribulation that are raised to rule with Jesus Christ in His kingdom for a thousand years. The unfaithful will not be raised at this time because their judgment, which had already taken place, marked them as unfitness to participate in the kingdom experience.

Three things must happen for the faithful to be given thrones upon which they rule with Christ during His earthly kingdom. First, they had to have died. Apparently, only immortal beings

---

[1] Cf., Lk. 16:19-25.
[2] That does not deny that this chronology is repeated in chapters 12-19 to explain many of the details that occur throughout the seven years, filling out the chronological details.
[3] Rev. 20:4-6.
[4] Rev. 19:11-21.

will rule with Jesus during His millennium kingdom.[1] The text specifically says that they had died. Second, when these were judged, they must have been justified,[2] qualifying them to be glorified[3] with Jesus in the earth's regeneration.[4] A person qualifies to rule in the kingdom by the godly perseverance given during his life.[5] Third, they had to be resurrected. The text says that they came back to life in order to rule with Christ. Only the qualified are raised, and only they rule. The wicked dead, those who don't qualify to rule, are not raised at this time.

The Resurrection of the OT Saints

Based upon Dan. 12:1-2 and Isa. 26:19, the OT Jewish saints who were faithful to God are raised after a time of intense tribulation unlike anything that has ever happened before in human history to enjoy *everlasting life* (i.e., eternal life*).* Matthew explained in his Gospel that this time of intense tribulation is the seven-year period of tribulation[6] predicted in the last days immediately prior to Jesus' return to earth. And the *everlasting life* that Daniel mentioned is synonymous to, Matthew assures us, the *glorious kingdom*[7] promised to David for the Jews.[8]

The three resurrections described thus far (and the resurrection of Jesus Christ in the first century AD), that of the believers in God's Messiah, Jesus, who constitute the church, that of the OT believers in Yahweh, and that of the tribulation believers

---

[1] Cf., 1Cor. 15:50.
[2] Rom. 8:30-34.
[3] Cf., Rom. 8:30-34.
[4] Cf., Matt. 19:28; Acts 3:19-21.
[5] Cf., 2Tim. 2:12.
[6] Matt. 24:21. This identification is assured if this passage is compared to Rev. 6-11.
[7] Matt. 25:34, 46.
[8] 2Sam. 7:12-16; Lk. 1:32-33; 10:25-28; Mk. 10:17-30.

continuing the faith of the church, together make up what the Bible describes as the *first resurrection*. Even though they are separated by seven years (or by over two thousand years if Jesus' resurrection is calculated into the time frame), in God's mind these together make up the first resurrection.[1] This is the resurrection of the righteous, those who were faithful in their God given stewardships while living upon the earth. The resurrection of the wicked apparently constitutes the second resurrection. Upon these the second death is experienced.

In the resurrection of church age believers, both the righteous and the wicked are raised together[2] even though only the righteous get to participate in Messiah's kingdom.[3] This same scenario of the righteous and the wicked being judged together will be true of *the two judgments of living individuals* although there will not be any resurrections involved in these judgments. Apparently, the OT people will have been judged before they are resurrected. Otherwise, there would be no basis for the resurrection of some but not all. In these four judgments, the righteous and the wicked are judged together even though only the righteous get to participate in the earthly kingdom of Messiah. Only in the resurrection of two groups of people are the wicked and the righteous *not* raised together (although they could have been judged together), the resurrection of the Tribulation faithful and the resurrection of the OT faithful.

The Judgment of the Living Gentiles

When Jesus returns to earth, He will gather *all the nations of*

---

[1] Cf., Rev. 20:4-5; 1Cor. 15:23-28.

[2] 1Thess. 4:15-17.

[3] Phil. 3:11-14. The resurrection that Paul was trying to achieve was an "out-resurrection" that identified him as one who had obtained the "prize" of kingdom rulership.

128

the earth and judge them as He had done with the nations surrounding Israel in OT times.[1] They will be judged based upon how they treated Israel in their times of distress.[2] Did they oppress them? Did they fail to support them when other nations oppressed them? Or did they come to their aid in their distress?

This judgment, like all the others named in Scripture, focuses upon an individual's works or deeds; it does not concern what they believed or in whom they had believed. *All the nations are accountable to the one, true God* who had revealed Himself to them clearly and, apparently, their responsibility to befriend Israel. How they treated Israel, the apple of God's eye, during her unparalleled tribulation will be the basis upon which they will be judged by Israel's God.[3]

It should be noted that this judgment, unlike the previous three, is *executed upon the earth rather than in heaven*. All those who are judged are in their mortal bodies; none have died; none have been resurrected for this judgment. The past lives of each of these persons and the past history of these nations will not be the focus of the judgment. Rather the basis of judgment will be how each person and nation treated Israel during her three and one half years of great tribulation. Belief in Jesus, the central idea taught by Christian leaders today, will not even be raised at this judgment. The treatment of Israel will either send a person into the kingdom of Messiah, now returned to earth to set up that kingdom or into a time of punishment even if a person had believed in Jesus previously.

---

[1] Cf., Obad. 1:10-14; Matt. 25:31-32.
[2] Cf., Obad. 1:15.; Matt. 25:40, 45.
[3] Matt. 25:41-46; Joel 3:1-2

The Judgment of the Living Jews

This judgment upon the Jewish people occurs at the return of Jesus to earth. While all the Gentiles are brought before Jesus in Jerusalem apparently, the Jews are taken into the wilderness for their judgment.[1] Having survived the horrors of the Great Tribulation during which two-thirds of the Jews and three-fourths of all human life were killed, these Jews will include both righteous and unrighteous persons. The righteous will be given the privilege of entering the kingdom of Messiah while the unrighteous will be prevented from participating in it. There is no mention of anyone being resurrected for this judgment.

The basis of this judgment like that of the living Gentiles is the works that each had performed. Had they been responsive to the revelation that God had given them during their lifetime? As God said through the prophet Ezekiel, those who *rebelled* and who *transgressed* against God will not enter the land. There is no mention of anyone dying because of his sinfulness. The only judgment seems to be exclusion from the land of Israel, the promised land. Hence, this judgment like all the others is upon the deeds or works that a man performed during his life. It is not based upon the fact he had believed in Jesus.

The Great White Throne Resurrection and Judgment

While there is a judgment upon Satan and his angels, that will not be covered here. Our interest is only upon the judgments that humans undergo. The Great White Throne Judgment is the last judgment and takes place at the end of human history.

This judgment is for all those who had not yet been judged

---

[1] Ezek. 20:33-38.

previously. That only includes the wicked Gentiles from the time of creation to the return of Christ, the wicked dead from the Tribulation, and both the wicked and the righteous who had been born after the millennial kingdom began. All of these will be judged after the millennium has ended and after the old heaven and earth have passed away completely but before the new universe has been created.

Those judged here will be judged *according to their deeds.*[1] Life is about what we do, not about what we believe. Incomplete doctrine or errant doctrine won't keep a person from enjoying God forever. What concerns God is whether each person chose to walk with Him according to the information that He chose to give to him. If he did, his judgment will go well. If he didn't, his judgment will go badly.

After all the judgments are surveyed, the main truth that must not be missed is this fact: *never is anyone judged on whether he had believed in Jesus.* The salvation that Jesus offered did not extend beyond the grave. My wife said it best when she said, "Jesus saves us for life!" By that she meant to affirm that Jesus saves us to live a life in communion with God as we represent Him in all that we do. She did not mean that Jesus saves us eternally. That concept is foreign to the Scriptures. How does your rap sheet look? Maybe it is time to respond to God's convicting work and do something about it.

---

[1] Rev. 20:12, 13.

Chapter 15

Salvation and the Kingdom

One of the most common mistakes that teachers make is to *assume* that the phrase *kingdom of heaven* is synonymous to the term *salvation*. Rather than repeating all that I have said in the previous two volumes of this series, I am going to simply take the apostles as exhibit A in a case against the possibility of equating the kingdom of heaven with salvation.

The apostles had believed that Jesus was the Messiah early in Jesus' ministry.[1] Having believed in Him as the Messiah, they were given eternal life[2] as they followed Jesus as the good Shepherd. This experience gave them power over all of their natural, spiritual predators and the realization of God's great love and care for them.[3]

But almost two years later, Jesus can warn these same men to whom He had given eternal life and with whom He had walked and served God that they were dangerously close to not entering the kingdom of heaven. The NASB translates this warning in the following manner:

> "Truly I say to you, unless you are *converted* and become like children, you shall not enter the kingdom of heaven." (Matt. 18:3)

This is an unfortunate translation because it misses the point of the warning completely. Not only does it mistranslate the Greek term, but it shows a misunderstanding of the relationship that

---

[1] Cf., John 1:35-51; 2:11-12.
[2] Cf., John 6:47.
[3] Cf., John 10:9, 11-12, 27-29.

exists between Judaism and Christianity. One ought to naturally ask the questions in light of the number of times that some form of this Greek term is used in the LXX and in the NT, "Why is it that only here is the verb translated *converted,* and why is it that it is never used anywhere else in the NT to describe what happens when a person (initially?) trusts in Jesus?" The point is this translation is special pleading, being theologically motivated rather than linguistically or contextually necessary.

If the term really meant *to convert* or *to be converted,* it should be obvious that the apostles had already gone through that process, whatever it might have included, almost two years earlier. They had already turned themselves toward Jesus; they had already believed in Him. And, on the authority of Scripture, it had *taken,* to use a medical metaphor.

But the fact is there is no convincing evidence that any such phenomenon was involved in anyone trusting in Jesus in the first century. *For certain, no Jew was ever converted when he trusted in Jesus.* Saul, who became the apostle Paul, puts this matter beyond debate when he says of himself in Acts 24:14-16,

> "But this I admit to you, that according to the Way which they call a sect I do serve the God of our fathers, **believing everything that is in accordance with the Law, and that is written in the Prophets**; having a hope in God, which these men cherish themselves, that there shall certainly be a resurrection of both the righteous and the wicked. In view of this, I also do my best to maintain always a blameless conscience both before God and before men."

What Paul is saying is that when he believed in Jesus, he didn't begin believing a lot of things that he had not believed before. He only put a name and a face to the description of the Messiah that he had already believed was going to be sent by his God, the God of Israel. To use Paul's *explicit* words:

"And so, having obtained help from God, I stand to this day testifying both to small and great, **stating nothing but what the Prophets and Moses said was going to take place**; that the Christ was to suffer and that by reason of His resurrection from the dead He should be the first to proclaim light both to the Jewish people and to the Gentiles." (Acts 26:22-23, emphasis mine)

Paul was not converted. He was illumined! He was given more revelation about the Messiah that he already knew was coming. But, by his own admission, he did not give up who he was or what he had previously believed when he trusted in Jesus. For more on this topic the reader ought to see the second book in this series, *Acceptable to God without Being Saved*.

The apostles had *presumably* already been saved (from hell according to evangelical theology) over two years before the time of the incident being described in Matt. 18:1-3. Nevertheless, by Jesus' own admission and warning, they could still miss the entrance into the kingdom of heaven. That means that the kingdom of heaven is not an equivalent to a one-time belief in Jesus (or to the reception of eternal life). It also demonstrates that the kingdom is still future. It had not been realized, nor had it begun to be so.

We teachers can be pretty tricky; hopefully it is never with the intention to deceive. But, when we are, it is always because we have been deceived ourselves. I remember reading a book entitled *The Presence of the Future*. It promoted the idea that the kingdom program of the Messiah is present today although its full manifestation was still future.

Tricky stuff! But to many a title like that given above or the idea suggested by it is self-contradictory. Something can't be present if it is future, and if it is future, then it can't be present. Even if this were possible, *the kingdom that is predicted in the OT*

135

cannot be manifested in parts, that is, gradually.

Those who believe that the kingdom is present and yet still future also would describe the apostles as being in the kingdom because they had been *presumably* saved, yet the kingdom of which they are a part had not materialized in its fullness. But the text doesn't make this distinction, does it?

Jesus told the apostles that, even though they had believed in Him and possessed eternal life already, they were in danger of missing the kingdom altogether. Jesus did not make a distinction between a spiritual part of the kingdom that had already come and a physical part that was yet to come. Jesus said that if the apostles did not humble themselves as a little child and stop fighting over the most privileged positions in the kingdom, they would not enter it at all. And He said it emphatically:

"You will *by no means* enter the kingdom of heaven!"

That is what He said, and when He said it, He forever distinguished the kingdom of heaven from Christianity's accepted, but incorrect, understanding of salvation. Believing in Jesus alone will not give anyone entrance into the kingdom. There is more involved. Grace and faith must be mixed with works or entrance, even for the *presumably* saved, is out of the question.

Chapter 16

No Other Name & No Other Way

Most children have played with the puzzles that hide words in a "square" of letters. The word can be written *vertically* ~ going from the top to the bottom or from the bottom to the top ~ or *horizontally* ~ going from right to left ~ or *diagonally* ~ going from the top left downward or going from the bottom left upward.

C	L	I	N	O	D	O	N	E	R	Z	T	C
E	O	D	O	R	K	A	G	I	S	R	O	T
V	U	M	N	R	V	B	Y	G	X	Z	W	M
L	G	O	E	S	I	E	C	E	P	T	L	R
O	E	I	R	S	N	L	S	T	K	I	X	S
T	O	I	T	H	E	I	F	A	T	H	E	R
E	U	W	U	K	V	E	N	H	P	E	E	W
P	X	I	K	A	Z	V	T	B	Q	A	B	S
E	X	C	E	P	T	I	I	A	V	V	N	J
E	I	B	E	A	R	N	L	L	O	E	Y	E
Q	V	N	O	P	E	G	W	R	I	N	D	S
U	E	H	X	R	T	A	K	J	F	B	X	U
A	W	I	E	S	C	N	Z	Y	R	Y	A	S
T	H	R	O	U	G	H	N	M	E	G	T	I

Nothing matters except finding the exact words that the player is looking for and that have been hidden within the *square*. The highlighted words represent John 14:6. Can you find these words as well: *heaven, believing, except, goes, none, Jesus, to, none, by,* and *in*? While they are similar to the highlighted words, they actually affirm more than the highlighted words do. Take a moment and compare the two sets of statements. Can you discern the difference in meaning between them?

That is a fun game to play with smaller children. Unfortunately, some approach Bible study in a similar fashion. They are looking for words or verses that *seem to say* exactly what they are looking for, and when they find them, they think they have verified the theological view that they went to the Scriptures to find. Being *predisposed* to find certain truths, they looked for verses that seem to confirm their theological propositions. Nothing else mattered really, except finding those words or concepts that *seem to say* what they are looking for in the first place.

That is called *eisegesis*, reading *into* the text what you want to find there. *Exegesis* is allowing the text to say what it says without forcing it to say what you are predisposed to find. Exegesis is natural IF we aren't predisposed theologically.

Because we are more theologically programmed than we think we are, we have to *unlearn* interpretations that we have been given for certain classic verses. We are going to look at two such verses in this chapter, John 14:6 and Acts 4:12. When their contexts are allowed to determine their meaning, we discover that these verses have been badly misused, creating a skewed world view that misrepresents both Jesus' purpose in coming and the world's greatest need.

No Other Way: John 14:6

In John 14:6, the contrast that must not be missed is the two ways or paths to the Father's presence. Jesus' path back to the Father's presence was going to take Him *through the death* on the cross. The apostles' path to the Father's presence, and every other person's by application, was going to be *through Jesus*. For the apostles their destination would be the same as Jesus'. But *the path* that they would take would be different and *the place* of their encounter with the Father would be different as well.

The apostles were *presumably* already *saved* individual[1] according to orthodox Christian belief. If that were true, then this verse could have nothing whatsoever to do with evangelism in the contemporary sense of the term. What is known for sure is this: the apostles had already believed in Jesus, had already received eternal life from Him (just as He promised each person who would believe in Him),[2] and had followed Him faithfully for three years.[3] The twelve apostles to whom Jesus made this statement hardly needed *evangelizing*.

What is the context? It is the context that ought to lead us in our understanding of the verse, rather than a theological predisposition. The context is straightforward. Jesus has been telling His apostles that He must go to Jerusalem and die.[4] But they were not open or receptive to that information.[5] Their lack of receptivity did not change the truth or change what was going to happen. It just made them vulnerable to spiritual attacks when the truth was being fulfilled.

The theme of the upper-room discourse is the fact that Jesus was, indeed, going away; He was returning to the Father[6] by way of the cross. Up to this point the apostles did not have to really deal seriously with this information, but now they were pressed to comprehend it, and that pressure caused considerable

---

[1] The *presumption* is based upon Acts 16:31 and Eph. 2:8-9. Most have been incorrectly taught that believing in Jesus at a point results in a salvation from hell and a place in heaven. Another *assumption* is that salvation and eternal life refer to the same thing, namely, an eternal destiny in heaven. That too is a mistake.

[2] John 3:16; 6:47.

[3] Cf., John 17:6-10; Lk. 22:28.

[4] Cf., e.g., Mk. 8:31-32; 9:30-31; 10:32-34.

[5] Mk. 9:32; Lk. 18:34.

[6] John 13:1, 3, 33, 36-37.

internal turmoil for each of the apostles. Peter, who had refused to accept Jesus' predictions of His coming death earlier in his ministry with Jesus,[1] now wanted Jesus to be specific about His *going away*.[2] He had been, of course, but Peter was simply not receiving that information until now.

Jesus told Peter that where He was going, he could not follow *at this time*, but he would indeed follow Him later. That was not good enough for Peter. He assured Jesus that he wanted to follow Him wherever He was going and was willing to lay down his life for Him. So, Jesus explained in more detail what was about to happen.

He was going away, that is, He was going to die on Calvary, and from there go to the Father (who was in His House in heaven). At the Father's House, He would prepare a room for each of the apostles so that they could be with Him. Hence, the apostles ought to have known both *where* Jesus was going and by what *path or way* He was going there. The *where* was explained again as going to the Father (who would be in His House in heaven) and *the path or way* was the death that He was about to experience. The apostles should have known these things since Jesus had been entirely clear, explaining them.

Since the apostles were not supposed to die yet, their path or way to the Father would be at *a different time* and possibly *in a different way* than the one Jesus was going to take. And importantly, it would be at *a different place* as well. As it turns out, the apostles all went to the Father's House the same way that Jesus did, namely, by dying physically. But that was not a certainty at this point in their lives. There was another option that

<hr>

[1] Mk. 8:31-33.
[2] John 13:36-37.

could have carried them there without dying. But that had not been revealed to any of them or anyone else at this time.

So now from verse five through the rest of the chapter and into chapter fifteen, the topic of discussion takes a turn. Jesus had been discussing how He was about to die and go directly to the Father who would be in His House. Since the apostles couldn't follow Jesus *at this time*, the Father was going to have to come from His House to them. He would have to come to them to make His *house or abode* with them even while they continued to live and minister upon the earth.

So, when Jesus gave His great *I am* statement in John 14:6 in answer to doubting Thomas' question, Jesus was explaining how the apostles could *go to the Father* without going the way Jesus was going or going to the place where Jesus was going to see the Father. Jesus was the epitome of the Father incarnated. As such He had given the apostles the opportunity to both *know* the Father and *see* the Father while they ministered alongside of Him. When He died, He provided everything that was needed to commune with the Father throughout the rest of their earthly lives. Consequently, Jesus explained to them that . . .

> "If anyone loves Me, he will keep My word, and My Father will love him, and **We will come to him**, and **make Our abode with him**." (John 14:23).

When we realize that the term *abode* here in verse twenty-three is the same term as that used in verse two and translated there as *dwelling places*, we see what Jesus intended to teach the apostles: *His time to die was at hand so He was about to go to the Father at His House in heaven; but their time to die had not yet come so the Father would come to them to make His abode (His house) with them through Jesus' provisions for them spiritually.*

Jesus' famous *I am* statement explains, then, how a person can *go to the Father* while he continues to live his life upon this earth. If he pursues the Father as Jesus explained in the fourteenth and fifteenth chapters of John's Gospel, the Father will respond and come to him and make His abode with him. The fulfillment of Jesus' *I am* statement is for those pursuing God in faith; it has no relation to the person who, for whatever reason, is not seeking God the way he should. And it is not *evangelistic* in the traditional sense of that term since it is for those already responding to God.

No Other Name: Acts 4:12

I was trained to view Acts 4:12 as an evangelistic passage in the same way as John 14:6. But when I began to renew my study of these passages, I saw that Acts 4:12, like John 14:6, had nothing to do with evangelism in the modern sense of the term. They both, along with the rest of the Bible, describe the possible benefits that can be experienced for anyone who was pursuing a relationship with God. The one, true God, man's heavenly Father, waits for His prodigals to return and sustains His faithful sons as they continue their walk of dependence upon Him.

I will always remember, with more than a little regret, the first time someone suggested to me that a person in the OT could have a relationship with God, one that was fully pleasing to Him, without believing in Jesus. Nick Kalavoda was a spiritual giant in my opinion and one who taught me as much by the way he lived his life as by the outstanding Bible studies that he offered through his radio program.

He first suggested to me in 1971 that Abraham was rightly

related to God without believing in Jesus. I won't go into the details of all the give and take between us and the rest of the staff team with whom I worked. But I do want to affirm that in my immaturity and lack of Biblical comprehension, I refused to believe what Nick was attempting to teach me from the Scriptures during that weekend retreat at Lake Rosemound in Louisiana.

All I could offer in response to him was Acts 4:12. It seemed so self-evident to me that no one, and I mean without exception no one, could be *saved* apart from Jesus because there was *salvation* in no other name given under heaven but the name of Jesus. That is what the verse says, is it not?

Like John 14:6, the clarity of Acts 4:12 was as perfect as any diamond that has ever been cut, and its meaning seemed unassailable. And I, for one, believed in the absolute infallibility of the Scriptures, and I still do. They can't lead a person astray IF they are properly interpreted and taken as a whole.

Back in those early days of the 70's, I hardly knew any verses of Scripture, and I certainly could not relate verses to the overall teaching of the Bible. I was vulnerable and completely dependent upon those who were teaching me the Scriptures. So, if they erred, I erred. If they were wrong, I perpetuated that wrong by following their teaching. It was as simple as that.

And these two verses are still used by most Christians today in exactly the same way that I was taught to use them: as evangelistic addresses to *the temporally lost and,* if their condition was not changed, *eternally condemned persons*. But as I demonstrated with John 14:6, the context of Acts 4:12 will show us that, in no uncertain terms, this verse has been misunderstood and misused for hundreds of years. We will discover that the errant meaning given to it, like that given to John 14:6, arises because it has been ripped out of its immediate context and made to address issues that were never on the mind of the original Biblical authors, John and Luke.

I am delighted to tell you that it was a layman in one of my Bible studies that first suggested that the context of Acts 4:12 definitively explains its proper meaning. I had already gone in the direction that my good friend was suggesting. But the context alone *forces* us to turn away from the traditional understanding of this verse. I had previously arrived at his conclusion from a word study on both terms *save* and *salvation*.

While I had not yet completed my word study to my own satisfaction, I had done enough to "see the handwriting on the wall." I now instinctively knew I had to look in another direction for the meaning of this verse. But Jim was ahead of me. He had studied the context closely and had become thoroughly convinced of its true meaning. What we found is amazingly simple and straightforward.

The context of Acts 4:12 begins back at Acts 3:1. This is the passage that describes Peter's and John's healing of a lame man outside the door of the temple. The central verses are these:

> "And when he saw Peter and John about to go into the temple, he began asking to receive alms. And Peter, along with John, fixed his gaze upon him and said, 'Look at us!' And he began to give them his attention, expecting to receive something from them. But Peter said, 'I do not possess silver and gold, but what I do have I give to you: *in the name of Jesus Christ the Nazarene, walk!*'" (Acts 3:3-6)

We ought to note the simple truth that *in the name of Jesus the lame man was healed*. The multitudes, going into the temple, were astonished by the lame man's healing and ran up to the apostles to inquire about this miracle. Peter clearly declared that it was not by their own power or piety that the lame man now walked but by that of Jesus whom they had crucified. But, Peter went on to explain, God had raised Jesus from the dead. To make sure that the gathering crowd understood the message he was preaching, Peter repeated himself, saying,

> "And *on the basis of faith in His name*, it is *the name of Jesus* which has *strengthened* this man . . . ." (Acts 3:16)

As Peter continued to preach, the Sadducees became troubled about the content of his preaching. They did not believe in a resurrection from the dead. So, on the basis of religious disagreements, they arrested Peter and John. These two would have to give an account of these activities the following day before, apparently, the entire Sanhedrin.

When the religious leaders brought them out from jail, they asked a simple question:

> "By what power, or *in what name*, have you done this?" (Acts 4:7)

To this question, Peter responded in Acts 4:9-10, 12, giving the exact same explanation that he had given to the crowds in the temple the day before:

> "... if we are on trial today for *a benefit done to a sick man*, as to how this man *has been made well [or has been saved!]*, let it be known to all of you, that *by the name of Jesus Christ the Nazarene . . . by this name* this man stands here before you *in good health. . . .* And there is *salvation [healing]* in no one else; for there is *no other name* under heaven that has been given among men by which we *must be saved [or healed]*." (emphases mine)

It is obvious that the apostles are on trial for healing the lame man the day before and for preaching in the name of Jesus whose power and authority had been displayed in the healing of this man. Both the healing and the preaching were done "in the name of Jesus." *The salvation that is being referred to is the **deliver-***

*ance experienced by the lame man **from his sickness**.* It is only in the name of Jesus that one can have the power and piety to heal, and then only when it is the will of God to do so.

There is no mention or reference anywhere in the entirety of these two chapters of a spiritual salvation from sins or from hell. To use this passage as an evangelistic invitation to the "lost" person is to remove it from its context, read into it the teaching that one wants to find there, and then to propagate more than the Bible actually affirms. *To conclude that no one can go to heaven apart from believing in Jesus is to misrepresent the teaching of this passage.*

The bottom line here is that Christians have taken a verse out of its context and created a false doctrine while, at the same time, they unintentionally hide or obscured a truth about healing. Salvation in this context is wholly about being healed of a sickness. This fact verse nine *forces* us to believe since it contains the same Greek verb as verse twelve.

The importance of this chapter of the book is seen in this fact: the possibility of going to heaven cannot be limited to believing in Jesus. He is not the way to heaven. He is *the way* of communion with the Father, and the name that has the authority and power to heal the body. Not only do John 14:6 and Acts 4:12 not teach that heaven is obtained only by believing in Jesus, but the whole Bible disproves it. This fact ought to change how we view those who have not trusted in Jesus yet. They need our help, but it isn't to get them to heaven. It is to get them through the difficulties of life with a *life* that only comes through Jesus.

Chapter 17

Salvation and World Religions

There is an obvious reason that this chapter on World Religions follows the last one which gave an exposition of John 14:6 and Acts 4:12. *Is the pathway to heaven as exclusive as we've been taught?* I am not denying or even suggesting that the exclusivity of the pathway to the Father's House or to His presence has changed. It certainly has not. But neither the pathway nor the salvation by Jesus' name is about going to heaven.

If these two passages don't restrict access to heaven to those who believe in Jesus, then where does that leave us exactly? And as I have shown in the last chapter, not only do those two passages not address the traditional concept of going to heaven, they don't even broach the subject of how one obtains a salvation from hell. Consequently, they don't require non-Christians to believe in Jesus in order to obtain heaven.

Western Christianity, especially since the Reformation, has hijacked Jesus and attributed to Him a purpose that He never came to accomplish. He never came to start a new religion, *the Christian faith*. He came to reinforce God's continuing commitment to the OT faith given to the Jewish nation. That is critical to understand.

The terms *save* and *salvation* are all about this present life and this life alone. We have been freed from the tyrant of sin within, rescued from the Devil without, and delivered from death, the consequence of living under either indwelling sin's mastery or the Devil's dominion. We haven't been saved from hell. No one has. We haven't been given heaven as a free gift. No one has.

The salvation of Mark sixteen is the reception of the Holy Spirit whose job it is to overcome indwelling sin within[1] among several other tasks as well.[2] The salvation that Mark refers to, like John after him, is more than a life of faith. The OT person pursuing God could live a life of faith. But they did not have the resources to live by the new life that Jesus came to grant each person who would believe in Him. *This life is the life of Jesus*, with all the communicable attributes that He displayed while He walked upon this earth. This life simply was not available until Jesus came into the world as the incarnate Son of God (i.e., the God-man). This life could not be obtained until the historical Jesus appeared, promising life as the result of one's faith. And that life was a *foretaste* of the kingdom that He was offering.[3]

This life is participated in or partaken of only by faith. That means that a person has three choices: he can live by his own resources; he can live by faith in God; or he can live by the life of Jesus, infused into him as he walks in reliance upon the Holy Spirit by faith. Which life are you living today? While there are other aspects to salvation, these are the pertinent ones relative to the other religions in the world.

Salvation through Jesus concerns additional resources to walk with the God who is revealing Himself to all men everywhere. This is the reason that Jesus needs to be preached to the

---

[1] Gal. 5:16-17.

[2] He will also lead (Gal. 5:18), empower (Acts 1:8), convict others through the communication of the good news about Jesus (John 16:7-11), help the student understand what Jesus meant by what He had taught (John 14:26), produce spiritual fruit (Gal. 5:22-23), manifest the life of Jesus within so that it could be said that Jesus was living His life through the one trusting in Him moment by moment (Gal. 2:20; Eph. 3:16-17), etc.

[3] Heb. 6:4.

148

rest of the world. People are hurting; they are struggling with life itself. They need to learn the good news that God has provided resources to draw close to Him. And if they do, God will bless them. But they don't need Jesus to go to heaven. They need Him to *deliver* them from the trials and spiritual defeats experienced as they live their lives in pursuit of God.

Because of a prevalent misunderstanding within Christianity about Jesus and salvation, most Christians think that the people of other faiths must be void of any relationship to the one, true God because they have no relationship with or belief in Jesus. It is impossible, they have been taught, to go to heaven without a belief in Jesus. Supposedly, this view is plainly taught by both John 14:6 and Acts 4:12.

But *what if* these verses don't teach such an exclusive mindset? *What if* these verses have nothing to do with going to heaven at all? And *what if* the terms *salvation* and *save* have nothing to do with the prospect of going to heaven? Where does that leave us? How do the Scriptures describe the rest of the world? It is past time to take an unbiased, non-theological look into this matter.

I am not going to try to be complete in this matter, for God knows that I'm not capable of being so. Nor am I going to cite the party line that I have been taught for most of my ministry. I will attempt to be as simple and clear as I know how to be, letting the Scriptures communicate whatever they want to say. At some point we must choose the Bible over our theologies.

Let's begin with Abimelech, the King over the kingdom of Gerar. This little episode had to have taken place very soon after God promised a son to Abraham and Sarah for she was not yet *showing* if she had become pregnant already. As Abraham was traveling with Sarah in Gerar, he told her to tell anyone who might ask her that she was his sister. Abraham's reasoning for Sarah to give such an answer is clearly revealed in Gen. 20:11:

> "Because I thought, surely there is *no fear of God* in this place; and they will kill me because of my wife."

That means that Sarah at the age of ninety was still looking really fine! In fact, she was so beautiful that the King of Gerar wanted to add her to his household! And the kings in ancient times didn't have to settle for anything but the best. This both the examples of Solomon[1] and King Ahasuerus[2] explain to us clearly.

Abraham's answer reveals more than an implication concerning Sarah's beauty; it also reveals the standard by which a person is *acceptable to God*. Abraham was afraid that there wasn't any *fear of God* among the people of Gerar. Now it goes without saying that Abraham was referring to the one, true God. Peter, the apostle of Jesus, infallibly explains the significance of Abraham's answer to King Abimelech when he said,

> "I most certainly understand [now] that God is not one to show partiality, but *in every nation* the man who *fears Him* and *does what is right* is *welcome* to (or *accepted* by) Him." (Acts 10:34-35, emphases, bracket, and parenthesis mine)

Peter had the same problem that Western Christianity has today: he thought that unless people came through Israel, they could not get to God. It was not until God gave him the vision of the unclean animals coming down out of heaven in a sheet that he was forced to rethink some of the *orthodoxy* that he had been taught throughout his life. Putting together the command to kill and eat some of the unclean animals and the ministry assign-

---

[1] 1Kgs 11:1-4.
[2] Esther 2:1-20.

ment of preaching Jesus to Cornelius, he began to understand how Jesus fit into God's plan. Now we're talking about an apostle of Jesus Christ! If he made this mistake after walking with Jesus for three years and being taught directly by Him, should we not expect it to be made by others as well?

To summarize: the Jews thought the Gentiles had to go through them to get to God; Christians think all non-Christians have to go through them (i.e., believe their preaching about Jesus) to get to God. According to both the example of Abimelech and Peter's clarification of the universal truths that result in acceptance by God, both are wrong. Generally speaking, there is no exclusivity in coming to God today or in going to Him in heaven later. The exclusivity lies in the pathway to eternal life and the indwelling ministry of the Spirit of God. Those come only through Jesus.

Next, we must ask ourselves this question, "Where did Abimelech and the rest of his nation, which is described as righteous by the infallible Word of God,[1] get such an accurate knowledge of the one, true God that it would produce a fear within them?" Let me give some bullet points of the truths that the Scriptures give to answer this question.

- **God is actively revealing Himself to all men**.

  "There was the true light which *enlightens every man coming into the world*." (John 1:9, following the wording of the Greek text closely.)

  "The heavens are telling of the glory of God;
  And their expanse is declaring the work of His hands.

---

[1] Gen. 20:4. You may have to check your marginal reference in your Bible for the correct translation.

Day to day pours forth speech,
And night to night reveals knowledge.
There is no speech, nor are there words;
Their voice is not heard.
Their line has gone out through all the earth, and their utterances to the end of the world." (Ps. 19:1-4)

- **This revelation is clear, being understood by all.**

"For the wrath of God is being revealed from heaven against all ungodliness and unrighteousness of men, who suppress the truth in unrighteousness, because *that which is known about God is evident within them*; for *God made it evident to them.* For since the creation of the world His invisible attributes, His eternal power and divine nature, *has been clearly seen, being understood* through what has been made, so that they are without excuse." (Rom. 1:18-20)

- **Yet, He is not giving the same revelation to all.**

"Men of Athens, I observe that you are very religious in all respects. For while I was passing through and examining the objects of your worship, I also found an altar with this inscription, 'TO AN UNKNOWN GOD.' *What therefore you worship in ignorance, this I proclaim to you."* (Acts 17:22-23)

- **His revelation is sufficient for a relationship with Him.**

"and He made from one (person, Adam), every nation of mankind to live on all the face of the earth, having determined their appointed times, and the boundaries of their habitation, that *they should seek God*, if perhaps they might grope for Him *and find Him,* though He is not far from each one of us ..." (Acts 17:26-27)

- **His revelation includes the notion of accountability**.

  "… so that they are without excuse." (Rom. 1:20)

- **That revelation foresees a day of judgment**.

  "And the heavens declare His righteousness,
  For *God Himself is Judge*." (Ps. 50:6)

  "… having a hope in God, which these men cherish themselves, that *there shall certainly be a resurrection of both the righteous and the wicked*. In view of this, I also do my best to maintain always a blameless conscience both before God and before men." (Acts 24:15-16)

- **His revelation may not include the good news of Jesus**.

  "And in the generations gone by *He permitted all the nations to go their own ways*; and yet He did not leave Himself without witness, in that He did good and gave you rains from heaven and fruitful seasons, satisfying your hearts with food and gladness." (Acts 14:16-17)

  "And also some of the Epicurean and Stoic philosophers were conversing with him. And some were saying, 'What would this idle babbler wish to say?' Others, 'He seems to be a proclaimer of strange deities,' ~ because he was preaching Jesus and the resurrection. And they took him and brought him to the Areopagus, saying, 'May we know what this new teaching is which you are proclaiming? For you are bringing some strange things to our ears; we want to know therefore what these things mean.'" (Acts 17:18-20)

- **God reveals Himself in many different ways**.

  Throughout the Bible God has revealed Himself and His

will in personal theophanies,[1] in dreams,[2] in visions,[3] in messages preached,[4] in written materials,[5] in signs and wonders.[6]

- **All men belong to God and are His sheep**.

"The earth is the Lord's, and all it contains,
The world, and *those who dwell in it*." (Ps. 24:1)

"Shout joyfully to the Lord, *all the earth*.
Serve the Lord with gladness; Come before Him with joyful singing.
Know that the Lord Himself is God;
It is He who has made us, and not we ourselves;
We are His people and the sheep of His pasture." (Ps. 100:1-3)

Acts 17:26-27 fits here as well! See its use above.

- **All men will give an account concerning how they lived their lives**.

"So then each one of us shall give account of himself to God." (Rom. 14:12)

"For we must all appear before the judgment seat of Christ, that each one may be recompensed for his deeds in the body, according to what he has done, whether good or bad." (2Cor. 5:10; cf., also Eccl. 12:13-14)

All judgments will be based upon what a person has

---

[1] Acts 7:2; Gen. 18:2-3
[2] Gen. 37:5, 9; Dan. 2:1, 28.
[3] Dan. 4:4-6, 9, 13.
[4] John 8:30.
[5] Acts 8:30-35.
[6] John 10:37-38.

154

done, upon his works alone. If they were carrying out the will of God and had been done in reliance upon God, then it will be openly declared that God is pleased with those works and has justified them and assigned rewards to them. If they were evil, wicked, or faithless works, these will be assigned by God a recompense as well.

I was taught that *the content* that a person believed was all important. A person had to believe the right content, or he could not be acceptable, received, or welcomed to God.[1] I realize that this is not only the methodology of seminaries, but also of denominations and local churches as well. So, for example, one denomination says that you must believe in Jesus alone to be saved from hell. Others say that you must believe in Jesus and persevere in your faith to be saved from hell. Still others say that you must be believe in Jesus and be baptized to be saved from hell. And still others say that you have to believe in Jesus and speak in tongues to be saved from hell. *They all mistakenly assume that being saved refers to escaping hell and going to heaven when a person dies.*

What a garbled mess we've made out of the message of the Bible. No wonder non-Christians remain unimpressed. And the irony is rather thick. While we can't seem to decide what is necessary to believe to go to heaven, we have decided that no one will reach that destination without believing in Jesus. It should be obvious why Christian Churches can't cooperate with each other in reaching other faiths with the message of Jesus: we can't decide what should be included in that message! We are fighting

---

[1] Unfortunately, it is traditional to use the terms save or salvation for this acceptability before God. *Being acceptable* to God and *being saved* are *explicitly* distinguished in the Bible (Acts 10:34-35; 11:14).

over the content instead of loving those in need.

Our theological debates have been used by Satan to keep us from working together to tell other people about the greatest message that they can hear in their lifetime. Giving people an assurance of heaven is not meeting their present need. Our ministries are well intended but ineffectual in laying a solid foundation for people to live abundant spiritual lives in the midst of their trials. We are trying to pull them through the trials but we aren't equipping them to be *more than conquerors through Christ*[1] who loves them and has provided all they need to live on a higher plane. Our focus and message must change to this.

---

[1] Rom. 8:35-37.

Chapter 18

Salvation and Evangelism

It should be obvious at this point that the template that I am suggesting for understanding the Bible demands a complete re-thinking of our evangelistic outreaches. *God did not send His Son to convert people.* Consequently, it should not surprise anyone that there is no reference of Jesus converting anyone! But He did rebuke, correct, and urge (almost) everyone to repent and turn back to God. That is the reason Jesus came. Turn back to God, trust in Jesus, and receive eternal life for living in communion with God. Trials will be overcome by the power and virtue inherent in the life that is received from Jesus through the Spirit.

Jesus didn't come to be the founder of a new religion. He came to His own people to give them resources that would enable them to live a life far above their own ability. His life in them could make all things new. His life in them could overcome every spiritual struggle that man ever has to face. His life in them can make even the most deprived life worth living.

Jesus came to offer this life to every person. *He was not offering to secure a place in heaven for anyone.* He was trying to secure an abundant, meaningful, and purposeful life now for everyone to enjoy. His new resources help the one living by them to face the growing intensity of the spiritual conflicts of life.

Sharing This Good News

To *evangelize* is to share the *good news*. That is what the term gospel means, good news. The Bible is filled with good news! Contention arises among us when we try to decide *what good news* needs to be shared and *for what purpose* we are sharing it. Not all the good news in the Bible has the same purpose unless we categorize it broadly under the rubric of walking with God.

What should be included in the message that we present to others? The answer to that question has been entirely dependent upon the religious tradition or denomination to which a person had been committed. Some have more content than others; some have additional obligations to fulfill than others; but all claim that their understanding is the correct one.

From my earliest days in the ministry, I discovered that I was expected to make a decision about water baptism. Was it necessary to be saved from hell? Then I discovered that I was expected to make a similar decision about speaking in tongues. Was this necessary to receive the Holy Spirit (and presumably to be saved from hell)? Still others outlined various additional doctrines that I was expected to believe in order to be saved from hell. These doctrines included the virgin birth of Jesus, the vicarious or substitutionary atonement of Christ, the Trinity, the deity of Christ, and so forth. If all this is more than daunting for the trained professional, can you imagine how the layman feels?

The fact of the matter is the Bible does not agree with the list that most theologians have created that supposedly must be believed in order to be saved from hell. The Bible makes it so simple that it is offensive to some. It only says,

> *"**Believe** on the Lord Jesus Christ, **and** you will **be saved**, you and your household."* (Acts 16:31)

Because that statement doesn't fit into many of the doctrinal statements that are presented to us, some try to force their preconceived ideas into the words used in this verse. For example, Paul said, *"Believe* on the *Lord* Jesus Christ."* So, tons of theological content are poured into the words *believe* and *lord* in order to support preconceived ideas of what is necessary to believe and what is the nature of the faith that must be possessed to be saved from hell. But to solve dilemmas such as this is exactly the reason that the Bible commands all believers to be diligent students of the Scriptures,[1] holding the recognized teachers of the faith accountable for what they teach.[2]

The fact of the matter is that there is more than one gospel given in the Scriptures. There is the gospel of God;[3] there is the gospel of the birth of Jesus;[4] there is the gospel of the earthly ministry of Jesus;[5] there is the gospel of the death of Jesus;[6] there is the gospel of the resurrection of Jesus;[7] and there is the gospel of the coming salvation of the Jewish nation by Jesus.[8] And most important of all, there is the gospel of the kingdom of heaven and the gospel of Christ[9] (relative to the setting aside of the Mosaic Law). To lead people into thinking that every time the term gospel is used it means the same thing is to mislead the people who want to draw close to God through the truth that He has given.[10]

The good news is intended for the whole world, and the fact that it has not yet been preached to the whole world must be

---

[1] 2Tim. 2:15.
[2] 1Thess. 5:12-22.
[3] Rom. 1:1, 2-4.
[4] Lk. 2:10-11.
[5] Mk. 1:1
[6] 1Cor. 15:1-5.
[7] Mk. 16:14-16.
[8] Rom. 1:16; 9:1—11:32.
[9] Matt. 4:23; 9:35 and Gal. 1:6-7; 4:21-5:1, respectively.
[10] John 8:30-32; 17:17.

weighed seriously. And since, after nearly two thousand years, it has yet to be preached to the whole, living world, (without taking into account those who have died over the previous two millennia without hearing of the good news of Jesus), we must consider more carefully than we typically do how such facts must bear on *the purpose of the salvation* that is being offered through Jesus. This is not good news for those who have never heard it! Do we care?

The Heart of the Gospel needing to be Shared

I had the privilege of breaking into the ministry through an organization called Cru. To say that Dr. Bill Bright was influential in my life would be to make an extraordinary understatement. While I don't know many who would have considered Bill a theologian, I would go on record today as one who believes that, while as staff members we had some confusion mixed in with our message, Bill's emphasis on God's love and forgiveness as related to this life is the best summary of the message of the Bible I have yet to be acquainted with. And I believe it is due to that message that God has continued to bless this ministry irrespective of the minor flaws that might be found in some of its teachings.

Cru's evangelistic booklet began with this statement: *God loves you and offers a wonderful plan for your life.*[1] God's love was verified in John 3:16. But the equally important part of the booklet's first point was that the plan God is offering was described in John 10:10b where Jesus said,

---

[1] CCCI's media foundation is now located at 375 Highway 74S, Suite A, Peachtree City, GA, 30269. It now prints newer versions of the first evangelistic tract entitled *Have You Heard of the Four Spiritual Laws?* It was written by Dr. Bright and used between 1965 and 2009.

"I came that you might have life and have it more abundantly."

This, I now believe, is the reason that Cru had such phenomenal success in the 60's and 70's when I was directly associated with it. The point of *the gospel is life*! A life that is given now to be experienced now! A life that changes everything as it maintains an intimate fellowship with God throughout the day! As my wife has so poignantly put it: each person that believes in Jesus is *equipped for life* ~ not for an interminably long existence, but for a vital relationship with the God of love and forgiveness now.

All people today need to know that the one, true God loves them and offers forgiveness for all that they have done in their lives regardless of how wicked or vile it may have been. God stands as the father of the prodigal son did in Luke fifteen, waiting and watching for His sons and daughters to return to Him. Out of His love, He offers forgiveness and life, the former relieves our guilt and shame, the latter makes available to us an experience that we have never had before.

We must remember that we are not seeking to *convert* anyone; we are seeking to draw them back to the Father's love, forgiveness, and care. They are related to us by creation, coming from the same family line, having been spoken to by God already, and loved just as much as we are. God is offering through our evangelism *new life* to the person we're sharing with. He is not offering a heavenly destiny of any kind. He is offering what is needed to make this life all that God wants it to be.

Evangelism is a Process

It should be noted that the passage identified by various editors of our English translations as "the Great Commission" is about *discipling* men and women *from every nation* under the sun.

Sharing the gospel is communicating to a person what he needs to know to return to God or draw ever closer to Him. And that is a process; it doesn't happen instantly. It is not the result of praying a prayer or of believing (as though these are different issues) a certain gospel message that supposedly includes all the right doctrines in it. Evangelism certainly has a beginning, but it has no ending. The distinction between evangelism and discipleship that we have made for decades, if not for centuries, is artificial. Both of these disciplines involve *enlightenment*, the communication of information that has not been previously known or received.

Initial faith in Jesus is simply the beginning of the discipleship process. After *eternal life* has been given, now *that life* must be lived, and there is much to be understood for that life to find its full expression. Hence, a person may believe in Jesus at some point, but he is to use the life given to him at that point to experience the love and power of God every day of his life. The reason that we have so many bewildered and frustrated Christians who are living defeated spiritual lives is that they believe that "salvation" can be boiled down to one response of faith that secures a heavenly destiny for them. But they are left to fend for themselves each day. If they can hang on, they will reach heaven eventually. That message minimizes the importance of God's design for this present life and how it relates to a person's final judgment.

In this process of learning, or of being evangelized (having good news taught to them), the whole Bible ought to be on the scheduled curricula for this training program. We must begin our teaching with the issues that are the most crucial to the people we are evangelizing. What are their needs? What does the

Bible say about those needs? These things are addressed along with the practical way a person lives by faith in carrying out his responsibilities before the Lord. Living by faith accesses the new life that has been received. All the content in the Bible is of no benefit at all if the way of walking by faith is not also explained. God is pleased only by a faith response. Without it we have no reason to think that we are responding as God desires and that He is somehow obligated to bless our responses regardless.

Summary

This message is actually very simple. Jesus came to bring additional *light* and *resources*. He didn't come to exclude anyone from the family of God. A person is in the family by creation. His inheritance is dependent upon his daily walk with his heavenly Father.

To the one who wants to add repentance to being "saved," I would say, "Fine. As long as we are speaking about the practical issues of working out our salvation with fear and trembling." To the one who wants to add confession or baptism or any other good work to being "saved," I would say, "Fine. As long as you realize that none of these things have anything to do with getting a person to heaven when he dies. Add what you will as long as the Bible commands it." Receiving eternal life from Jesus is by grace through faith alone. But living by that eternal life involves obeying whatever command God has set before us. The whole message of the Bible is this: *Fulfill your divine commission of having constant fellowship with God as you represent Him in all that you do.* With that God will be pleased and you will be confident to stand before His Judgment Seat in the day of judgment. *A wasted life now can't be remedied by a dead bed confession of faith in*

Jesus. Enjoy Him now in the day of grace, and you will never have a reason to be concerned in the day of justice.

www.ingramcontent.com/pod-product-compliance
Lightning Source LLC
LaVergne TN
LVHW051059080426
835508LV00019B/1960